To my father, John Paul Bocchi, my hero. Thank you for everything. Without your legacy, none of this would have been possible. I love you and miss you every day. Rest in peace.

SWAY

MATTHEW JOHN BOCCHI

A POST HILL PRESS BOOK
ISBN: 978-1-64293-860-9

Sway
© 2020 by Matthew John Bocchi
All Rights Reserved
First Post Hill Press Hardcover Edition: September 2020

Cover design by Vendela Larsson
Author photo by David Genik

All people, locations, events, and situations are portrayed to the best of the author's memory. While all of the events described are true, many names and identifying details have been changed to protect the privacy of the people involved.

Post Hill Press
New York • Nashville
posthillpress.com

Published in the United States of America

AUTHOR'S NOTE

This work is a memoir. It is a true story based on my best recollections of various events and experiences in my life. In an effort to deliver a story both accurate and readable, I have recreated dialogue, included only the most interesting events, and in a couple of instances conflated two or more actual people into a single key character. I've also changed nearly all personal names and identifying characteristics, company names, and many locations to protect the privacy of those portrayed.

INTRODUCTION

I WAS EIGHT YEARS OLD when my father invited my younger brother Nick and me to his company Christmas party at Cantor Fitzgerald. The bash was held on the 105th floor of One World Trade Center in Lower Manhattan, where my father had an office. Ironic that he worked so high up given his fear of heights. Most people forget that, for a brief moment in history, One World Trade Center was the tallest building in the world. According to my mother, my father was obsessed with the disaster movie *The Towering Inferno*—the fictional story of the tallest skyscraper in the world set ablaze, destroying the building and killing many of those trapped inside.

Early in the party, my father walked us to one of the narrow, floor-to-ceiling windows and stopped several feet short. He pushed us ahead of him. "Go on," he said. "Look down."

Nick and I put our noses to the cold glass and tilted our heads forward and looked.

"We're twelve hundred feet up," he said. "You feel it?"

"What?" I asked.

"Look at the people on the street."

What I saw were dark specks moving along the sidewalks, a group of specks crossing the street. The cars appeared like toys.

"What?" I said again. Then I felt it—a slow rocking motion, the building itself swaying in the wind.

1

As a boy, I was oblivious to the push and pull of global forces and extremist ideologies, and everyday dickmongers who couldn't control their urges, and how oxycodone and Xanax and cocaine made everything better—until they didn't. On the other hand, I knew how I felt on September 11, 2001, and the days that followed, and how those feelings solidified or expanded...or whatever feelings do after years of rumbling around inside a body.

My father, John, met my mother Michele while they were both working at a law firm. My mom was a secretary, and my dad worked in the mailroom. They were friends until one day my dad showed up in Brooklyn, where she lived.

"I'm in Brooklyn. Do you want to go to the movies or what?" he confidently remarked. He took her to see *Commando,* starring Arnold Schwarzenegger. Soon enough, my dad proposed to my mom at Windows on the World—the restaurant on the top floors of the World Trade Center. Two and half years later, they were married.

My dad was told that he wouldn't succeed on Wall Street because his last name ended in a vowel—turns out a man born from poor Italian immigrants didn't garner respect from the waspy types. "We'll see," he said, and eventually worked his way up from the mailroom to the top of one of the biggest brokerage firms.

Eventually, my parents had four boys of their own—me (the oldest), Nick, Michael, and Paul. Paul's birth completed our family in June 2001. They had everything they wanted: my dad was successful at his job—as managing director of interest rate derivatives at Cantor Fitzgerald—and even had his favorite sports cars. Most importantly, they owned a beautiful house—rather, a home—to raise four young boys, and life was content. But it wouldn't last for long.

My brother Nick and I attended Harding Township Elementary School, a public school and a good one, I think. Fifteen, sixteen kids to a teacher. Pre-K to eighth grade. I was a fourth-grader. Nick, a second-grader.

Around nine o'clock on 9/11, the superintendent of schools, Dr. Marino, stuck his bald head in my classroom, scanned the room, then walked in and whispered to my teacher, her back to the room, all hush-hush. Marino was a good guy, a hint of a smile perpetually plastered on his face. He was a disciplinarian when he had to be, but even then, you weren't mad at the messenger. You got caught was all.

When my teacher, Ms. Lewis, pointed at me and another kid, Sam, and motioned us to the front of the room, I was pretty sure we'd been caught. For what, I didn't know.

Ms. Lewis was young, early twenties, favored sweaters with high collars. She was likeable, though sometimes unsure of herself. She glanced at Dr. Marino and then at the door, hesitant, mulling over whatever goes through the head of a fourth-grade teacher, and finally walked Sam and me to the door. Behind me, I sensed Dr. Marino stepping forward, saying a few words I didn't catch, warming up for what I was sure was a catchy monologue about keeping the playground free of M&M wrappers.

When we arrived at the corridor, standing there was the second-grade teacher, Ms. Green, and my little brother with a concerned look but still smiling, a gap showing between his two front teeth—and Sam's younger brother Brett. It occurred to me then that Sam and Brett's father worked in the same building as mine.

Ms. Green, it seemed, was in charge, and she led our little troop to an empty classroom four doors down and waited until we boys had all taken seats.

Then she spoke. She assured us that both of our fathers were safe.

I looked over at Nick, who stared back.

"Nothing to worry about," Ms. Green said. "Really."

"Why are we here?" I asked.

Then she told us there'd been an accident, or not an accident, exactly. Or, she wasn't sure. Forget that part. An airplane had crashed into one of the towers. The north tower. Her voice was higher than usual, strained with lots of pauses, searching for the right words. She told us the authorities were evacuating the building. Nothing at all to worry about. Even as she spoke, I wasn't fully paying attention. I was sneaking glances at Nick, his dark hair combed straight up into a kind of inverted cone, his

3

shirt buttoned right up to the neck. I thought about the pilot—
the kind of trouble you'd get into for flying into a building.

Ms. Green glanced at Ms. Lewis. In hindsight, these two
were just a couple of kids a year or two out of college. Not really
grownups. Not yet.

"Any questions," Ms. Green said.

It wasn't really a question. Even at nine, I knew the difference
between a question and a statement, and this was a statement.
You have no questions, am I right?

Sam shook his head. Brett, too.

Brett was a thoughtful kid, narrow face, crooked teeth. The
kind of kid you wanted to pat on the back, tell him it would be
okay even if you knew otherwise.

Ms. Green waited.

I shrugged, turned to Nick. He shrugged back.

Then, abruptly, we were escorted through the door, into the
corridor, and back the way we had come. My fourth-grade classroom had windows into the corridor. As Sam and Brett and Nick
and I ambled past, every kid in the class stared at us. We were on
display, sort of like zoo animals, the stare suggesting they knew
something we didn't. In the back, I saw my best friend give me
one of those big toothy grins. His name was Connor Fitzgerald, but everyone called him Fitzy. He waved, his hand close to
his chest, kind of hiding the gesture. Up front, Dr. Marino was
wrapping up, rubbing his hands together, smiling at his audience
of nine-year-olds.

We arrived at another empty classroom—the computer room,
as it was known. Each of us played the computer game *Gizmos
and Gadgets,* for what seemed like eternity.

After a while, we returned to our classrooms. For the next
few hours, the kids in my class just sat there doing nothing.

Ms. Lewis did her best to get us back to normal, but her heart wasn't in it. Even if it was, every few minutes the door opened, a mom stormed in, spotted little Patrick or little Claire, and off they went. One by one, our classmates were taken out of school.

Even Sam and Brett were eventually plucked from their respective classes and carted away.

By lunchtime, it was just Nick and me, him in one classroom, me in another. At first, I wondered why *we* had to stay in school. Then I got angry that we were the only ones left in school. Whatever was going down, I wanted out. I had a bad feeling. An airplane crash, evacuation, lots of blubbering mothers snatching up their kids, grabbing hold of tiny wrists, and not letting go. *Our* father worked in the World Trade Center. If anything, we should move to the front of the line.

Eventually, Nick and I climbed on the school bus. The boxy thing was empty. Not a soul except the bus driver, a heavy man with sad eyes, Nick, and me. The bus driver motioned us to hurry along. We sat, two small kids in the same seat, eager to get home. A mile and a half and five minutes later, we got off the bus at the end of our street and began the walk up the hill to our house.

I could see that the normally quiet street was filled with cars. As we got closer, I saw that our driveway itself and even the lawn were jammed with cars and SUVs parked at odd angles. The setting looked rushed and chaotic, like a crime scene on *Law & Order*.

Our house was big and white, likely some version of Colonial. Rectangular. Symmetrical. Lots of double-hung windows with small, equally sized square panes and green wooden shutters. If the original Colonial house was a single clapboard-sided box, then ours was the upscale New Jersey version—four giant boxes connected, the boxes turned this way and that, all of it sitting in the middle of a massive green lawn. There was something wholesome and patriotic about it. We even had a flagpole out front flying an enormous American flag.

We walked in the back way, through the garage and into a long hallway. At the other end of the hall was the living room, and I could already see it was filled with people. Aunts and uncles and grandparents and neighbors and other people I didn't know. A few steps closer, I saw my mom's cousin, who I called Aunt Ann, talking to Grandma Laura. There was Hamilton, a former colleague of my father with some degree of sketchiness about him, leaned against the door frame. I stopped at the kitchen door and saw Fred and Kathleen from across the street, and Margaret, Daisy, Hanna, and some others—all friends of my mother's—standing around the kitchen table. Everyone amped, no one sitting for some reason.

In the TV room, Mrs. O'Brien sat on one of the plaid couches scowling at the television, the sound as loud as it would go, along with a dozen or more other people watching the news footage of airliners colliding with the towers.

Mrs. O'Brien was the mom of a kid in Nick's grade. Every few moments, she'd turn away and tighten her lips, angry and willing to show it, *wanting* to show it. She'd had enough news but lacked the oomph to get up and move on.

When I looked at the television, I saw a person jumping, floating ever downward, and eventually, the towers collapsing—the south tower, and seconds later, the north tower.

I learned later the towers didn't come down within seconds of each other. Instead, the south tower collapsed at 9:59 a.m. with the north tower a half hour later at 10:28. Not that it mattered. To me, it all came crashing down in one fluid motion—one then the other. In addition to the footage of the planes and falling towers, I watched other images, a collage of video and photos, each more unthinkable than the last. I saw people running away from the collapsing towers, and a woman fall or jump from the building. Why would she do that? Doesn't she know the firefighters are coming to save her? I heard the newscasters talking, over and over in a loop. When it ended, the loop started again.

Many of the people in the living room were on the phone, some dialing my father's cell phone, others calling hospitals throughout the tri-state area. In the kitchen, I heard people dialing hotlines set up to identify and locate missing family. I watched Nick walk away from the TV to join them.

I stood and stared at the TV. He'd be okay, right? My father way up near the top of the building—a building that no longer existed—but he'd gotten out. Right? He was alive. Right? He'd be home soon, put on a big smile, shake some hands, and then shoo all these people out of our house. Or we'd all have a party, eat, celebrate—I didn't know what.

Someone turned the channel. An uncle, I think.

On-screen, I saw the north tower still standing. A woman's voice in the background saying something obviously devastating has happened, though her sources couldn't say exactly what. Old news. What I saw was a gaping hole in the building. Thing was, I knew that building. Knew how ginormous it was, and that stupid hole was what, only five, six stories tall? Maybe five times that wide. I'd been up close to the tower countless times, knew the architect's name: Something Yamasaki. I'd also been on airplanes a bunch. That chasm in the tower wasn't caused by a Cessna or a Piper or even one of those enormous jets, a Gulfstream. I saw the opening but no sign of the airplane. The tower had absorbed it, swallowed it whole, and for a moment, the tower looked even bigger, the gash smaller. Inconsequential.

Then the loop continued and one tower came down. Then the other.

There had to be a way out. No way he didn't get out. I needed him to get out. He needed to come home.

I knew the kind of person he was—smart, resourceful, a man of character, a man for which everything eventually panned out. He found a way out, I was sure of it. Hell, not only did he get out, he carried injured people down flights and flights of stairs. In my mind, my father was a hero.

Grandma Laura, my mom's mom, had Nick by the arm, and she pulled him toward me. She told us to go over to the Kellys' house. Noah Kelly was my age, and I often crossed our backyard into his and knocked on his door.

Grandma sort of waved at the back lawn. "Go on," she said. "They're expecting you."

"I want to wait," I said, meaning wait for my father to get home.

"It's going to be fine. Go play."

It was warm outside and windy. As Nick and I trudged across the backyard, I wasn't all there. I was dreamy, absentminded. I was in shock. I'd seen the news footage but didn't believe it. In a way, I didn't believe any of it. I repeated to myself: *the Twin Towers were too big, the airplanes too small. All those people didn't really jump. The towers didn't really collapse.*

That our entire family and friends and a few strangers had gathered at our house comforted me. They were adults. They'd work it out. They'd find him. They'd convince him to come home.

Only, he didn't come home.

Not that night.

The following day, Wednesday, people flooded the house, arriving early—filling every room with noise and speculation and lots of crying. Nick and I took turns calling my father's cell. Someone had left the old Panasonic cordless on a small table in the foyer. I grabbed it, dialed, got my father's voice telling me to leave a message, so I did. "Hey Dad, it's Matthew. Please call me when you get this message and come home soon. I love you." I handed the phone to Nick. "Your turn." We left one message after another, begging him to come home.

If Wednesday was weird, Thursday was weirder. People, some strangers I didn't know, showed up at the front door, knocked, then walked right in. The mood was lousy, and each newcomer only made things worse. Some nitwit turned on the television and we all stood around watching the same people saying the same things, the same images in the same sequence—airplane crash, smoke, building collapse. Over and over. I remember staring dumbly at the television, the sound off, the soundtrack provided by the voices and conversations throughout the house. I singled out my mom talking to someone in the other room, telling whoever it was that they'd find him. No way they wouldn't find him. They'd dig him out. A pause, as I imagined whoever it was nodding or frowning or both. Then, she said, he'd come home. Others repeated her words, the part about digging him out, and each time I heard it, I sensed a smidgen of conviction slipping away.

What struck me was the consensus that my father was somewhere beneath all that steel and smoke and throat-choking dust now on the ground. I didn't think my dad was under all that rubble. I knew he found a way out before the building fell. How would he breathe with all that dust and steel covering him?

As the day wore on, people turned sulky, cantankerous. Some arguments flared up. There was lots of crying. I'd never seen so many teary-eyed, sobbing adults in my nine-year-old life.

That night there was a prayer vigil at our house. Father Paddy organized the gathering for just after sunset. It was chilly, in the low fifties, but there was a calmness in the air that gave it beauty. More than a hundred people showed up all holding candles and trampling our massive front lawn. Some friends and family and lots of people I didn't know. It felt like half the town had shown up. Father Paddy said a few words, then a prayer and another prayer, and when he took a breath, someone started reading the names of the missing.

My family gathered on the front porch. Each of us held a lit candle, and we listened to the names, pronounced slowly, loudly, enunciating each syllable. All of a sudden, the dark sky was brightened with lightning and a single burst of thunder. I learned years later that in that moment, my mom felt something and accepted that my dad was safe. She turned to Grandpa, whispered *he's not coming home.*

On Friday I woke early, ran down to the kitchen, grabbed the phone, and called my father's cell. Earlier that year, he'd lost thirty-eight pounds, mostly from pumping iron before work at a gym. I later learned this was called The Fitness Company— member number WTC18221—adjacent to the Marriott hotel and next door to the north tower. He was in great shape, muscly. He looked to me like a young Arnold Schwarzenegger, the early version in movies like *Commando* in which Arnold played a retired Delta Force operator. Even as I dialed, I pictured my father—strong, athletic, even brawny, trapped beneath a million tons of rubble, all that splintered wood and sheet metal and asbestos and watches and wedding rings. I imagined him climbing upward through the rubble, pushing chunks of concrete and rebar and bits of office furniture out of the way, so he could get up and out of the heap. He'd follow the sunlight, hold his breath so he didn't gag on the dust and smoke, and he'd reach the top of some jumble of twisted metal and take a big breath of air. Then he'd make his way to West Street or Vesey Street, or one of the other streets that bordered the World Trade Center complex. He'd find Greenwich Street and walk north, against traffic, and he'd keep walking, blocks and blocks, and—I don't know— maybe he'd board the PATH train and zoom under the Hudson River to Hoboken, then onto Journal Square where he left his car. He'd climb into his Porsche—a silver 911 Carrera—and race home. Any minute now, he'd walk in the door covered in dust. He'd stink of smoke. Oh, and he'd have a box in his hand from Lenny's Pizza over in Bernardsville—half cheese, half pepperoni—like he carried into our house each Friday night for as long as I could remember.

"Dad please, please come home. We miss you and want you to come home. Can we drive in the Porsche when you get home? It's Matthew. Okay, I love you."

I played this idea of Arnold-Dad over and over in my head, elaborating, adding details, and changing tiny elements of the story. I needed the narrative to make sense.

I took it a step further, reenacting the scene with my younger brothers Nick and little three-year-old Michael—Mike. One of us would be Dad, the others a fireman, or a cop, or maybe a Good Samaritan. Whoever chose the role of firemen would put on ski pants, baggy nylon overalls that resembled the heavy yellowish bunker gear worn by real firefighters.

When I was Dad, I'd lay on the ground surrounded by fragments of the old towers—pillows and blankets and tipped-over chairs and whatever else was nearby—and I'd lay there shouting for help as Nick and Mike dug me out. "Hurry," I'd say. "I don't have long. Faster. Faster."

"We're moving as fast as we can," Nick would say.

"Move faster!"

"Stop shouting at me!"

"I'm under here!"

Each time we reset the game, we'd argue over who would play Dad.

And each time we started over, we'd make the pile of rubble a little higher, a little more complex, more pillows, more couch cushions, some cardboard boxes from the garage stacked so they might tip over at any moment.

2

I WAS ONLY NINE YEARS old, but I knew what death was. It was the end. When it came to my dad though, no amount of rational thought could outweigh my feelings. I watched the footage over and over again, trying to validate my hopes and dreams, believing there was a minute possibility he made it out of the building alive. And when the day came that I was told my dad wasn't coming home ever again, it just initiated a new, deeper search for answers. His death was just the beginning.

On Tuesday, September 18, 2001, two cars eased up the drive. I stopped playing football with Nick in the foyer and watched through the narrow front window as a police car and a dark black Nissan turned into our driveway and moved tentatively forward and parked. Four people got out—Mr. Daly, a local police officer; a man and woman in spiffy dark suits who looked like they belonged in *Men in Black*; and Father Paddy O'Donovan from the church we attended—Church of Christ the King, in New Vernon—who was close friends with my father.

Father Paddy came over for dinner at our house with my grandparents one time. He and my dad drank red wine and made jokes the whole night that guaranteed I couldn't stop laughing. I had wanted to stay up late with them, but my father finally gestured for Nick and me to go to bed with his sarcastic "time for B-E-D, bed," phrase.

Now, Grandma Laura appeared in the foyer and said, "Matthew, Nicholas, go upstairs."

"What's going on?" I asked.

"Now," she said.

"But Father Paddy—"

Her face was pink. She pointed up the stairs and shouted. "Go up." Then turned and shouted even louder, "Michele!"

Nick and I trudged up the stairs, stopped on the landing, and sat where we could see part of the front door.

Even before the men knocked, Grandma opened the door. My mother then appeared in the foyer, patting down her shirt, pushing hair out of her tired face. Grandma stood behind her, nudged my mother forward, but held onto one arm. I could see a man's pant legs.

"Mrs. Bocchi. Michele."

I knew the voice—Officer Daly, soft-spoken, no wasted words. We lived in a small town, a township of seven hundred people or so with a handful of police officers. Everyone knew the man in charge.

Mom said, "Tell me you found him."

"These men here with me—" Officer Daly paused, couldn't get out the words. "They've identified John's remains."

Then my mother shrieked or squealed, the sound our dog Fritzie would make when we stepped on her tail by accident. "No!" she screamed, her body sliding down the edge of the dining room wall.

Grandma helped her up and squeezed her tight—her face flushed and sprinkled with tears.

Father Paddy stepped forward. "Michele, we're very sorry."

Mom composed herself. "Remains?" she asked.

One of the prosecutors, I think, cleared his throat and said, "The toothbrush and hair samples you provided, they're a match to your husband's DNA. I'm very sorry."

"When?" she asked.

"Pardon me?"

"When did you find him?"

All I could see was feet, but the feet shuffled around, one prosecutor looking at the other, conferring without saying a word. The one in front turned back to face my mother and said, "The fourteenth. Friday."

"You said remains?" she asked again, her voice cracking.

Officer Daly shuffled sideways for a moment, and I caught sight of a bowed head.

The woman prosecutor stepped forward, whispering to my mom. "My understanding is they found his lower half."

"What do I do? What am I supposed to do now?" my mother asked, her sobs overpowering her words.

"Doyle Funeral Home is a great place. They are a very nice family. A lot of people in town use them," the woman prosecutor remarked.

I had never seen my mom cry that way before, and I knew something serious had happened. What exactly, I didn't know. Maybe my dad was in the hospital and badly hurt or something. Or maybe they had to cut one of his legs off because he broke it so badly. He was definitely still alive. I knew that for sure.

Not long after, my mother found Nick and me sitting on one of the steps near the top of the stairs. She glanced up at us, her eyes red. She waved her hand. "Come with me."

"Where?" I asked.

Too tired to argue, she turned and walked slowly down the hall.

We followed her into my father's office at the end of the hall. She was first through the door, and I heard her footsteps loud and hard on the wooden floor. Another kind of wood on the walls, dark and grainless. The room was large, a big old-school desk in the middle, a credenza pushed against the wall, and between them, a red leather desk chair, tufted, with the buttons pushed deep into the leather. My father loved that chair.

She said, "I have something to tell you." Then she stopped and looked around the room, kind of swiveled her body in a half-circle, and in that moment, something let go inside—her body slumping or shrinking, getting smaller before my eyes.

She'd been quiet so long, I asked, "What?"

She said, "Go on," and gestured to the desk chair.

Nick and I both wanted the red chair, so I sat, and Nick wrestled his way next to me.

My mother glanced off again, maybe at old photographs on the shelf. She said, "Daddy isn't coming home." She turned and looked at Nick, then me, tears flooding down her cheeks.

I didn't hear the words so much as feel them. I started to cry. Mom moved closer—down on her knees, leaning forward to hug me.

Nick just sat there, a big question mark on his face, unable to take it all in. Finally, he said, "My dad's dead?"

"Oh, honey," Mom said.

"He isn't coming home?"

She shook her head.

"Ever?"

Another shake.

Then Nick hopped off the chair and walked out of the room.

I sat there and cried with my mom for a bit. She didn't know what else to do besides hug me and kiss my head.

The following morning, I called my father's cell phone and left a voicemail. I begged him to come home. An hour later, I did it again. And again, until his inbox couldn't receive any more messages. When I heard the beep, sometimes I just cried. I wanted him to hear me cry. I wanted him to know we cared, and I'd run out of words, so I cried. After a few times, I'd call and leave no message at all but listen to the silence, really listen, for some code or hint in the hiss of the line.

I remember being at home the next night, out back, close to the house, throwing a football in the air, chasing after it, and occasionally catching it before it hit the grass and went bouncing away. It was dark, or half dark, and I could barely make out the ball against a colorful sky, a hint of orange and red.

I had on my New York Jets jersey, hunter green, "Chrebet" stitched in white letters across the back. The jersey was a gift from my father. I loved the Jets. He favored the Miami Dolphins like a lot of Wall Street types. No telling why. I'd just thrown the ball in the air. I looked up, and out of the corner of my eye, I saw the shadow of a man leaning against the wooden arbor that separated our driveway from the backyard. The arbor was a simple four-post structure, some decorative beams, and latticework across the top, all of it connected to a white picket fence.

17

I chased after the ball, caught it, told myself I'd imagined the whole thing. By now, I stood in the deepest part of the backyard, way past the leafless dogwood, closer to the swing set. It was dark outside, or at least darker. I threw the ball in the air a couple of more times, then stopped and took a hard look at the arbor. He was gone. I threw the ball, caught it, looked up, glanced side to side. There he was over by the swing set, my father, easy as you please, just standing there watching me. He wore work clothes—a suit and tie—and was smiling with his arms crossed.

"Hey, Dad."

No response.

"Dad?"

Nothing.

"You can say something, you know."

This time I didn't wait for a response. I threw the ball in the air, watched it for a moment, and let it fall. I looked over, and he had disappeared again.

I left the ball in the yard and jogged to the back door. Just inside, I saw Mom standing next to the window. She asked, "Who were you talking to?"

"Dad," I said. "Over by the swing set."

"Honey..."

"He didn't say anything."

"Sweetie."

"I know."

It didn't occur to me that I wouldn't see my father again for quite some time. I had no idea that without him by my side, I was soon to embark on a journey into hell. More importantly, however, I didn't know that he would reappear in my life when I would need him most. Not in human form, of course, but reincarnated as a fly.

Of course my father didn't *want* to die. He wanted to come home.

But he didn't. He couldn't.

I laid on the green plaid couch in the TV room, my feet and shoes on the cushions, and I prayed, I mean really prayed, that he'd suffered a head injury, a big one, some piece of steel had come swinging down from above like in the movies and bashed into his head. A loud *clank* as it hit. I could almost hear the clank. And the bash made him forget who he was, forget where he lived, and it wasn't his fault he couldn't find his way home.

I watched the television, and someone said they weren't digging up any more bodies, not intact bodies, at least. The rescue crews were down so deep—fat chance they'd find a whole person. At this point, it was just lots of parts. I learned later that tens of thousands of body parts were recovered and only 293 intact bodies, a tenth of those killed that day.

The weeks after 9/11 were a blur. People coming and going, the front door hanging open much of the time, people I didn't know piling in, hands filled with baked goods and casseroles and all kinds of stuff. The food was okay. The people less so. They wanted to talk to me, to chat, to make me feel better. Or maybe they just wanted to make a connection of some kind and always fell short. What could you say, especially to a nine-year-old whose father was just obliterated? "How's school going? Do you like your classes?" The forced conversations became repetitive and annoying and so I would just wander off in the basement to play *Madden NFL 2001* or *FIFA 2001: Major League Soccer* on my PlayStation 2.

I wanted to be alone, just me and my thoughts, caught up in a confusing nightmare I was sure would end soon. Even after the funeral, I thought I might wake up from it.

A day or two later, Mom told someone his remains were cremated. It finally occurred to me that this was real. That image of my father bashing through the rubble, his muscles and arms bulging with vascular veins, became instantly squashed. What was even left of him anymore now that my mom had him cremated? Some well-meaning people would tell me he would live on in my memory, for me to think of the good times and all that. But I strained to remember them.

My mother waited in the foyer and shouted upstairs for us to get a move on. Nick was at the top of the stairs, his white dress shirt unbuttoned at the neck, the tail in back sticking out of his pants. "Do we have to?" Nick asked.

"Yes, honey. In the car."

I was downstairs, holding the front door open. I said, "We already went to one of these things."

"That was the funeral mass. This is the memorial mass."

The funeral mass was a week prior at Church of Christ The King, with eight hundred people or more in the pews. Uncle Tony stood up front at the wooden podium and gave the eulogy. Tony reminded me of my father. His upright posture, the suit jacket buttoned up, the way he used his hands when he spoke. He talked about how my dad was a hard worker and always put his family first before anything. He talked about their love of Ferraris. "Accelerate into the turns, Tony!" my dad would always say while driving his Ferrari 348. He said more about how my father was an inspiration to all those he encountered. There were many lessons to be learned from my dad's short-lived life, and part of his legacy was providing my family a life he never imagined possible.

A memorial mass, I learned, was a service to honor the deceased when the body was cremated, or perhaps vaporized under two hundred thousand tons of steel.

For this particular mass, the church offered a two-for-one: my father, John Paul Bocchi, and Matthew Sellitto, another Cantor Fitzgerald employee and New Vernon resident who died on 9/11. I liked Matthew. He was a cool dude—young, only twenty-three, hired months earlier as a trainee to work in the company's interest rate derivative group under my father. My father took Matthew under his wing, even convinced him and his brother Jonathan to come over one weekend and help paint our pool shed out back. I pictured my father and Matthew together way up in the towers, smoke everywhere, hot steel making creaking noises, Matthew looking to my father for guidance on how to get out of there.

Grandma Laura stood in the foyer looking stern. "In the car. We're late."

Me and Nick and Mikey climbed in the back seat of my mom's Lexus SUV. Little Paul, only a few months old, strapped in his car seat next to Mikey. Mom and Grandma up front, frowning in the rearview mirror as if they knew what was ahead.

The First Presbyterian Church of New Vernon was founded in 1883, a white building, Greek Revival, big windows. We walked in and sat in the front pew. The place was packed. I hated being there. I glanced around, embarrassed, saw a bunch of kids from my elementary school class staring at me.

The choir started up with "Amazing Grace." When I heard the first few notes or chords or whatever they're called, the music took over and I cried.

I was the center of attention.

A big baby with big baby tears.

I felt judged, pitied, I didn't know what.

I hated the way the other kids looked at me, hated the way they talked behind my back. Some of the kids, their parents were divorced. Divorce was expected. Divorce was normal. I was the kid with a dead dad. On 9/11, no less. Not normal. I was the only kid in my class without a father. He'd never be there for a soccer game, never sit quietly in the audience for a school play.

The day before, some girl in my class said, "I'm sorry for your loss." What kind of kid says that? She said, "I know how you must feel."

No you don't.

I was pretty good at soccer, short and quick, the ideal stature for a forward. My favorite soccer player was Alessandro Del Piero, a forward with Juventus F.C. Even as a kid I tried to style my play after Del Piero's own quirky style, scoring goals any way I could. My father made a habit of attending games, always shouting encouragement, sometimes coaching the team.

I loved and hated when he coached me, often pointing out what I could do better. *Never give up on chasing the ball. Always play until the whistle is blown.* He had a talent for directness and kindness at the same time, and I could hardly muster the anger to talk back, even when he reminded me I was playing like shit.

That first season after 9/11, I was one of Harding Township Rec League's leading scorers. In our championship game against one of the Madison rec teams, I scored two goals. The second was one of my best. I took a pass from Nicky DiCenzo, did a swift dribble past one of the defenders, and let the ball get ahead of me. The goalkeeper sprinted to the ball, but before he got there, I darted forward, deked, drawing him out of position and poked the ball in the lower corner of the net.

I glanced into the crowd, half expecting to see my father cheering me on.

Except he wasn't. He didn't. Whatever.

After the game, Coach Kelly came up to me. "Great goal, Matt. You played like a champion."

"Thank you."

"You know, your dad was scheduled to coach with us this year. He'd be very proud of you."

3

IN THE MONTHS AFTER 9/11, my mother was physically present. Emotionally, not so much. She was always crying either on the couch or in her room. Most of the time, I would comfort her; other times, I just wanted to get away from her. When I would go hang out with my friends, Fitzy and Nicky, it annoyed me how their families were so perfect. They had dads for one, and mothers who weren't upset all the time. I felt bad leaving my brothers home with Mom. And it would only get worse.

We began therapy with a woman we were told to call by her first name, Amy, an outdoorsy type, wiry-strong with large teeth and lines around her eyes. She gathered us in a small room in a yellow building. Amy and my mother chatted away. Mom told her about the call from the medical examiner, a hurried man full of facts, she said. He said the blood wasn't deeply absorbed into the muscle tissue, an indication my father's death was quick. No suffering. No asphyxiation. No burning. He was alive one moment and dead the next, and even then it sounded phony to me, a little white lie meant to console, perhaps, or just memorized lingo used with all the wives.

Most days, we'd all show up together, my mother and me and Nick and Mike and even little Paul. As brothers, we knew the drill. We'd push through the door and sit on the floor and play games. Or, we'd pull a handful of games—Robot Turtles and Dixit and Jenga and a pile of others—from the mountain of boxes stacked neatly against one wall. Paul was around nine months old, still a crawler, and particularly adept at yanking one box after another from the stack.

Sometimes we'd just sit around a low coffee table and eat pretzel rods from a plastic tub Amy kept in the middle of the table. Flour and salt and malt syrup. What's not to love? Other times, Amy gave us a pad of lined paper and ink pens someone had already chewed on and encouraged us to draw whatever came to mind.

"What are you drawing, bud?" Amy always called me bud, probably couldn't keep us boys straight.

"Nothing, I guess," I said.

"Tell me about it."

"The towers, is all."

The drawing was simple, maybe a dozen lines to the whole thing. The first airplane was already disintegrated into the north tower, no airplane visible but a mass of squiggly lines representing the flames and smoke moving across the tower sort of parallel to the ground. I drew a second airplane approaching the other tower from the right of the paper.

"This?" she said, pointing at a stick figure with a very large head.

"A jumper," I said.

"And this?" She touched a line on the page that connected the two towers.

"The Marriott. It's a hotel."

I'd drawn one unlucky soul jumping to his death, soon to land on the roof of the Marriott hotel next door. My uncle Sal was dating a woman, Becky, who worked at the Marriott. I overheard her talking about how she was there that day, she arrived via the World Trade Center PATH station, stopped at a deli at track level—the one with the best yogurt muffins in the city—and took the escalator to the mezzanine level, a Banana Republic store straight ahead, a Duane Reade, a Sbarro, that's when she heard the first airplane hit the tower behind her, she had no idea what it was, an explosion, and the panic, everyone running, a huge cloud of white dust falling like fine snow. Sal tried to get a word in, said it was papers and stuff—meaning the dust—but Becky wanted to talk, wanted to tell it without stopping, without periods, told him *no, no, no,* that was later after she hit the street, the mass chaos and just huge chunks of concrete on the ground and then people, that was all later. The talk turned to jumpers—or maybe it was another conversation, another time, didn't matter—some hitting the roof of the Marriott, twenty-two stories off the ground. Thirty, forty people, who knew how many for sure, and the devastating noise a body made as it landed on something hard and flat—glass and blood everywhere.

That was a conversation I wasn't meant to hear. But I did.

"Why draw someone falling out of the buildings?" Amy asked, watching as I illustrated the towers.

"It's not a faller."

I drew a version of this same image many times. And each time Amy pulled from the same playbook, asked the same questions, used the same shrinky tone, as if she was curious is all. Just asking.

Another time, I answered differently. I was in a mood, I suppose. "Because," I said, "that's what they did. They jumped. They couldn't get out, so they jumped."

Once I overheard Mom telling Amy they'd found most of him. All but his left arm. They had recovered his lower half months ago in September, then the upper half, minus the arm, in October. She said she'd gone into the City and someone had made a sketch of all the parts they recovered. It was mostly all there but the one arm. Five years later, she got another call. Someone in the medical examiner's office said they'd found rib bones and some tissue stuck to the bones.

We were a diligent family and made our weekly appointments with Amy. Did so for several months, and in that time, little changed. I continued to look at these 9/11 books my mom got that had timeline pictures of the day, and I recreated my drawings from those pictures. More burning buildings, more people falling, more questions, no answers. Mom knew Amy from town, her own kids attended Harding Township Elementary School, so eventually, Mom figured it best to widen the circle.

Next up was Dr. Weber, a real doctor this time. She was easier to make fun of because she had a small dot on her face, and Mike and Nick and I would turn our backs and whisper, "Moley, moley, moooley," stretching out the word and mimicking an absurdly funny scene from *Austin Powers*.

Dr. Weber didn't do a lot of talking, something they must teach at NYU School of Social Work. Instead, she used lots of "Mmms" and "Ohhhs" to get her point across.

Every other week we kept coming back. When my turn came, just the doc and me one-on-one, I'd talk jumpers—why they jumped, how they jumped, what happened to a body when it hit. In our family sessions, I'd draw on a little child-sized whiteboard or yellow memo pads I thought of as therapist paper. I'd draw lots of things, but every few drawings I'd manage to sneak in a jumper or two, sometimes obscuring the image so you might think it was a bird or a piece of colorful confetti caught in the wind.

I was a huge Yankees fan because of my dad. In April 2001, he took Nick and me to opening day against the Red Sox and said that he would continue to take us to as many games as possible that year. The 2001 World Series was pushed back because of the 9/11 attacks and didn't start until the last week of October. The Yankees were playing the Arizona Diamondbacks, but most of the country was rooting for the Yankees—it was seen as a symbolic moment for the city of New York, as well as the country. My gym teacher had gotten tickets to one of the games and offered them to me, an extremely nice gesture to say the least. At the last possible minute, my mom wouldn't let me go because of some apparent bomb threat at the stadium. I don't know if there really was or if she was just overly paranoid given the circumstances, but regardless, I had to stay home and watch the game on TV.

I watched one of the games in the family room, wearing this New York Yankees satin bomber jacket my dad got me and my Yankees hat, holding my dad's oversized glove, daydreaming of catching a homerun ball. I pictured myself on the first base side of the field, right above the dugout, getting autographs from Derek Jeter and Bernie Williams. Even more so, I thought about my dad somehow trudging his way from the rubble at Ground Zero all the way to the stadium, his button-down sleeves ripped from the effort. He would have blood dripping down his massive arms, and his pants and shoes would be covered in dust from the debris. He would scream my name over the loudspeaker and come limping to find me and pick me up, holding me on his shoulders, and we would drive home in his Porsche.

How did he die?

For years, from those early days after 9/11 to my twenties, I chewed on this one question.

They found him, or most of him, at least. So he was definitely dead. Still didn't answer *how* he died. Something I was desperate to find out, no telling why.

Did he breathe in great gobs of smoke and pass out from lack of oxygen? Did he somehow sense what was coming—the building collapse, his own life coming to an abrupt end—and rather than panic, politely usher everyone to the stairwells in an orderly fashion, then stand to the side until the iconic structure folded in on itself and he was crushed by all that mangled steel?

Or, did he, just maybe, jump?

Was my father one of many who broke open a narrow, eighteen-inch-wide window, squeezed past the shards of glass, looked down a quarter mile or so to the street below, and jumped?

I was fourteen when I started down a rabbit hole of my own making, a hole so meandering and convoluted it would take me years to resurface. I wanted to know if my father jumped, and to answer that question, I scrutinized thousands of photos I found on the Internet. I googled "9/11 people jumping" and a hundred other similar search phrases.

I sat at the desk in my bedroom. The room was intentionally dark, with just a small lamp with an even smaller bulb next to my computer. First, I found a close-up photo of the north tower, several dozen people hanging out the windows. I spent hours staring at that one photo, zooming in as much as I could to get a closer look. I used several digital magnifier programs I stumbled across online to enhance the photo, to omit some of the graininess, to make the people more recognizable.

Then I wandered across a government website, vaed.uscourts. gov, and found a case titled United States v. Zacarias Moussaoui, Criminal No. 01-455-A, a real find, that one. The website had a listing of Prosecution Trial Exhibits. Moussaoui was the jerk who federal prosecutors believed was a replacement for the other nineteen jerks involved in the September 11 attacks. Moussaoui was the second string. Not good enough to make the A team, but he'd do if anyone balked and he had to come off the bench. In the end, he admitted to being a member of al-Qaeda and more or less copped to all the charges.

Moussaoui's trial generated hundreds of exhibits, thousands maybe—video clips, transcripts, ABC's *Nightline* news video, passenger lists, bank statements, not to mention photographs.

I must have clicked through hundreds of photos—security camera stills, unflattering images of Moussaoui, several of his low-life terrorist buddies and their unnerving grins, a yellow-handled box cutter, the fronts of several scruffy apartment buildings, a stucco house in Florida painted baby blue, the high-res image of a squarish white flight simulator for a Boeing 727.

Farther down the webpage, I got to the photos taken after the attacks.

The exhibit descriptions were bland—intentionally dull, was my guess. The first description I came across said, "Photograph taken on September 11, 2001, of a human body part located at the intersection of Albany and West Streets in Manhattan." The body part in question was far in the distance, seventy feet or more from the picture-taker, impossible to recognize, a spot of reddish something or other in the middle of a dull gray street.

Digging further, I came to the close-ups. Hands, feet, legs, most so squishy and mangled the parts were nearly impossible to recognize. I had this crazy notion that if I could identify an arm or leg, a shoe, a suit jacket, a familiar-looking tie—anything belonging to my father, in other words—maybe there'd be some way to put all the pieces together. Close to three thousand people died that day, and I was trying to locate the pieces of one man who worked on the 105th floor. Made no sense. I know that now. I knew it then. Nevertheless, I eyeballed photo after photo, sifting through a mountain of data hoping for a single clue.

Then came Exhibit 200011.

I took a quick tentative peek, then sprinted to the bathroom and barfed in the sink. After, I looked at myself in the mirror, washed my hands and face with some flowery-smelling soap. I brushed my teeth. I returned to my computer and settled in for a good long stare.

Hard to know what I was actually looking at, but in my mind, it was a person lying face down on the street. The bottom half of the body dressed in a dark suit, likely expensive, the upper half an explosion of bright red guts—liver, lungs, intestines, and whatever else comes churning upward through the skin when a body spats on the hard asphalt at 125 miles per hour. From the angle, the head might or might not have been missing. Definitely, one leg was gone, or perhaps the leg was twisted underneath the parts I could see.

I watched a video, a newsreel that seemed to focus on jumpers, a slick-looking reporter talking to a round-faced man who described the bodies hitting the pavement as ripe tomatoes; then a New Yorker with a heavy accent looking for someone to blame, and a blonde woman who thought she saw trash falling from the sky only to realize the large pieces of trash were jumpers, the woman bawling as she spoke, gasping for air, her words coming more slowly until she was too distraught to speak.

Some of the photos made me sick. Others made me cry.

A few sent me into a kind of prolonged shock. Like the one of a single jumper, a person, caught in time against the backdrop of white vertical lines, the perimeter columns, and the dark grey of the windows. In some of the windows you could see lights, maybe desk lamps or ceiling lights or conceivably emergency lights, the kind that automatically kick on during building evac. The photo was cropped so you couldn't tell which tower. The whole thing was fuzzy and disorienting. But in the center there was clearly a man, arms and legs spread like a skydiver, his grey shirt and undershirt riding up his belly. No shoes. The man was falling face down. He sees what's coming, and it's this last part, the seeing that bothered me most. Why fall face-forward? Why not fall ass-first? Why not look up into the blue sky, the white clouds, or just shut your eyes and dream of a better place? Why are so many jumpers straining their heads and bodies, contorting themselves into ungodly positions, to see what's coming?

Then I thought: This pixilated person could be my father.

And the more I thought about it, I knew my father would do the same.

John Paul Bocchi would face what was coming head-on.

Every once in a while, my mother would sneak into my room. Not sneak exactly, just open the door, uninvited, and walk in. She could even be noisy about it. I wouldn't hear a thing. I'd be engrossed, back to the door, hunkered down and hunched forward, all my attention on my Apple iMac, a massive screen, or so it seemed at the time, in a moon-white frame. Maybe she bought me the computer to avoid having to see "9/11 jumpers" in the family search history all the time. I wanted more information, faster. I wanted clearer images, bigger, colossal. I forever searched for some new photo or video, anything related to 9/11 I hadn't seen a thousand times before.

Often when she showed up, I was glaring at a body part, trying to decipher precisely what I was looking at.

Eventually my insides hardened, or steeled themselves, or whatever insides do to prevent you from upchucking when confronted with grossness on a grand scale. Thereafter, no photo was too gruesome. No image too repulsive.

Behind me, she'd speak softly; tell me I was making myself crazy. She might even joke about it, a put-on happy tone. Not an order to stop, no way it was an order, but it sort of felt that way.

I never hid my research, never made any effort to keep my actions a secret.

That said, I didn't advertise it either. I'd sit in my room for hours, alone. And the part about being alone was important. I needed to do this by myself. I didn't want my mother to be a part of it. She didn't understand what I was going through. How could she? When she made any effort to stop me, hinder my progress in any way, no matter how well-meaning, I took it personally, which is to say I got angry. I had a right, didn't I?

"Honey," she'd say.

"I know what you're going to say."

"Why are you looking at that stuff?"

"I knew it."

"You realize this isn't helping?"

My back still to the door. "You're making me mad."

"Not my intention."

I'd fume for a few moments, conjuring up something clever or just mean, then let loose. "Clearly you could give two shits."

"Matthew John, that's not fair."

Just the mention of my middle name—my father's name—was meant to pull me back in line. Never worked. I said, "I really don't care what you have to say."

"You're only hurting yourself, honey."

"Mom, would you please just leave me alone? You don't get it. Whatever you're about to say, whatever it is just fucking stop." My dad would kill me if he heard me talking that way to my mother. I knew she only meant well, but it didn't matter to me. I would put her through much worse before I came to that realization.

This was about the time she'd met Joe, a goddamn plumbing contractor, for chrissake. A good guy by all accounts, two equally good kids of his own, but none of that mattered to me. My mother had moved on. She was over it, all of it. Maybe she wanted to give my brothers and me a new father, I don't know. No matter who it was—or what they did for a living—no one could ever replace my dad.

She'd once told me she would never look at the gore I dredged up, the pictures and videos, because she was afraid she'd come across something so, I don't know, ugly, appalling, it would taint her memory of my father, the way he was before, some image so terrifying it might overwrite whatever nice memories she'd stored away for the long haul.

She didn't back off. She spoke, her voice almost a whisper. "Do you want to talk about the nightmares?"

Did I mention the nightmares? They were recurring. Three of them.

In the first, I'm on the ground level of the north tower, in the lobby looking up at the mezzanine level and the mass of people shuffling forward. At ground level, policemen and firemen with black gear and yellow helmets stand next to the stairwell exits shouting at people to rush to the lobby doors. Other firemen prevent people from clogging up the works by running into and up the stairwells. The elevators are locked down. No way I can make it up one hundred and five floors to save my dad. I'm stuck, frozen in place, it feels like. Every few minutes, I hear a crash, more of a blast, and everyone ducks or hunches, like turtles, a reflex, as bodies land in the plaza or on the roof of a building nearby. I'm facing the mezzanine and each time the sound hits, I watch an older woman with white hair involuntarily put her hand to her mouth, holding back puke or tears or I don't know what.

In the second dream, I'm on the 105th floor, standing next to one of the open windows, smoke everywhere, my father beside me, his arm around me, pulling me close, both of us leaning forward looking down at the ground below. The window glass is missing and I take my father's hand and we move to the opening. Behind us, a long line of colleagues is ready to take our lead. We crawl out and I feel the wind in my face and we jump. I open my eyes right before we hit the ground.

In the last, I'm once again on the 105th floor, my father a couple of steps ahead of me, walking confidently to one of the open windows. I can't do anything to stop him from jumping. No matter which dream scenario my brain decided to play out, each resulted in the same ending—waking up in a state of utter panic and horror, gasping for air.

4

At some point, I switched gears. Rather than focus on how my dad died, I wanted to know how long he suffered. So I set out to create a timeline, a list of events that day involving my father, or at least the most probable series of events. It began to fall into place with the stories people told: my mother, Uncle Tony, one of my father's colleagues.

On September 11, 2001, my father climbed into his five-year-old Porsche and drove to the PATH station at Journal Square in Jersey City, parked and boarded the train for the ten-minute ride to work. He arrived at Cantor Fitzgerald early, took the underground concourse to the north tower, climbed aboard an elevator that took him to the sky lobby on the 78th floor, got off, and walked a short distance to another elevator that shot him up to the 105th floor and to his office.

There he began to prepare for the markets to open by contacting clients.

He called Peter Galanos, both a client and a friend. The two met five years earlier when Galanos joined a trading desk at a client of Cantor Fitzgerald's, Bear Stanley. Galanos had moved on since then and was now a senior vice president with LRD Capital Markets, a long-established capital markets firm in Greenwich, Connecticut. They often talked of family, specifically about me and my younger brothers—little Paul, Michael, Nicholas—two fathers sharing stories. After a minute, they moved on to interest rate deposits and treasury bonds and swapped transactions and over-the-counter rate options. A check in about life, then business. Old school.

The line went dead.

The intercom crackled. A woman's voice, low-key, unflappable, announced that the building had been hit by an aircraft. Most likely a small airplane. *Everyone, please move to the stairways and evacuate the building in an orderly fashion.*

Many Cantor Fitzgerald employees were in the building eight years earlier in February 1993 when two morons, Ramzi Yousef and Eyad Ismoil, drove a yellow Ryder van filled with thirteen hundred pounds of urea nitrate–hydrogen gas explosive into the parking garage beneath the north tower. Yousef lit the fuse, and the two men ran for it.

The 1993 bombing confused and disoriented thousands of people who worked in the tower but, except for the loss of six poor souls, the catastrophe was cycled through the media relatively quickly. A small aircraft crashing into the building was likely no different. Best to move to the stairwells and begin the long hike down to the ground level.

As others were gathering their belongings, my father pulled his cell phone from his pocket and dialed my mother.

She was at home in the TV room, sitting comfortably on our old plaid couch, breastfeeding my baby brother, Paul, only ten weeks into the world. She hefted Paul, and the two hurried to the kitchen where she snatched up the cordless telephone, a clumsy black Panasonic, next to the sink. The caller ID flashed my father's cell number. She pressed the button, heard the normal rustling and commotion in the background.

She was surprised by the call. My father never telephoned before the markets opened. Her initial thought was that he was calling to let her know he'd finally quit his job. He'd had enough, was ready to pay down the mortgage as they'd talked about only days earlier and find a new position, maybe a whole new career, one that was a lot less stressful.

He spoke quickly. "Do you have the TV on? We think a small plane hit the building."

She tried to slow her breathing. "John, this better not be some kind of sick joke—"

My dad liked to play practical jokes, so it wasn't surprising that she didn't believe him. She heard a hazy white noise, some clicking on the line. "Hello? John?"

The line went dead.

She hurried back to the TV room, grabbed the remote, and pressed the power button. On-screen, she saw the Twin Towers, the distinctive white vertical lines of aluminum-alloy, and pale gray smoke billowing from the side of his building. A numbness paralyzed her body when she saw how much smoke there was.

He kept calling but the connection was horrible and filled with static. She redialed his cell number. Then redialed again. Nothing—the lines were busy and she was flooded with panic.

Back in the TV room, the phone in one hand, baby Paul pressed to her chest, she was suddenly tired, exhausted, her arms throbbing. She squatted and placed Paul in his infant seat, a Fisher-Price sit-me-up, sky blue with large orange and red squeezy toys strapped to the sides. Then she called my father's mother, Elena Bocchi, Nonna to me.

"John called. He thinks a small plane hit the building," my mom repeated.

Nonna reacted as one would expect—hysterically screaming and crying once she saw the scene. They both watched the images of smoke billowing out of the north tower on the television. The news was rushed and conflicting, pretty people with white teeth yammering on incessantly with little or no new information.

People poked their heads and bodies out the windows, fleeing the fire, gasping for air. One floor above my father's office, on the 106th in the restaurant Windows on the World, people waved tablecloths out the windows. *I surrender*, they seemed to say.

My mother was horrified, the phone to her ear, watching. One of the news anchors confirmed that American Airlines Flight 11 had crashed into the north tower at 8:46 a.m. A short seventeen minutes later, another flight, United Airlines Flight 175, flew into the south tower at 9:03 a.m.

My mother hung up with Nonna and again telephoned my father.

The calls went to voicemail. *You've reached John. Please leave your name and number, and I'll get right back to you.*

Then the phone rang. "Michele," my father calmly said, "I don't know if you can hear me. I want you to know you're the love of my life. I'll love you forever."

"I love you," she shouted into the phone. She began to scream uncontrollably.

For the second and final time, the line went dead.

She called him back several times but couldn't get through. The lines were still busy and eventually went dead. Each time she mentioned how much she loved him, not knowing if he ever heard her.

Anthony Bocchi, Tony to his friends—Uncle Tony to me, woke to the sound of Nonna screaming. He jumped out of bed and ran upstairs, where he found his mother standing in front of the television, near-hysterical, sobbing and shouting at the boxy set and its faux wood veneer.

Tony didn't speak. Instead, he stared at the television. On-screen, he saw the northeast face of the north tower, a fiery glow from the flames, more an odd-shaped orange fireball, a kind of curved series of flames following the downward angle of the airliner's impact. Just around the corner on the southeast face, massive plumes of ugly white-brown smoke floated upward and appeared to smother the building. As he stood and watched, the white-brown smoke slowly turned black.

He knew one thing instantly—my father, just a few floors above the crash, wouldn't survive.

At the time, Uncle Tony lived at home, fresh out of Rutgers and about to start nights at Seton Hall School of Law. He worked at the law firm Pillsbury Winthrop as a law clerk—a job my father helped him get. Pillsbury's New York office at One Battery Park Plaza was just blocks from the World Trade Center. On his daily commute via the PATH station five floors below street level at the trade center, he often arrived early and shot up the elevators to visit my father. On Tuesday, September 11, however, he never made it into Manhattan. He skipped work to prepare for law school orientation on Wednesday and Thursday, and the first day of classes on Friday.

Tony ran into the kitchen and dialed my father. He tried the office line and when he got no answer, punched in his cell number. Nothing. No ring, no busy signal, not a sound. He dialed again and again and again. Nothing. He paused, took a breath, and started over.

Just as he was about to give up, my father answered. "Hello?"

According to Uncle Tony, he sounded...well, normal. Just another day at the office, as if Tony was ringing his big brother from downstairs in the lobby, something he'd done hundreds of times. The calm tone, Tony believed, was my father's way of consoling a younger brother in this moment of terror.

Tony shouted into the phone, "John, get out!"

A pause. "Tony, I love you."

Then the line went dead.

The call didn't last ten seconds.

Just then, my grandfather, who we called Nonno, walked in the front door and into the kitchen, fresh from eight o'clock mass at the Church of the Epiphany in Cliffside Park. He could walk it in ten minutes but always drove—his daily endeavor. Nonno looked at Tony, both men concerned. Tony was unable to speak so he pointed to the den, shorthand for *Mom's in there*. He didn't want to tell my grandparents about the call. Let them hold out hope, even for just minutes. Tony stood there in the kitchen for another moment, then ran downstairs to the basement, out of earshot, and cried.

That out of the way, he dialed my father's cell phone and left a long voicemail.

He promised to take care of my mother and us boys—the youngest ten weeks, then three, seven, and me, nine—to teach us how to act as honorable and good-natured men like my father. He would do what he could, he said, to protect us, to be there for us, to impart life lessons, to give us a shot at maturing into normal, functioning human beings in this cold world. He pledged to encourage us to harness all of the negative energy swirling about into something good.

Thanks to my relatives, my timeline extended back a few weeks before 9/11, back when my father called Tony and said he'd found this joint in Englewood. A bar, a lounge, he didn't know what to call it. "You got to see this place," my father said.

"It's a Tuesday night," Tony said.

"Come on. Let's get a beer. A five-minute drive."

John, my father, was fifteen years older than Tony. Growing up, the age difference had been an issue, but lately, the gap had narrowed. My father had the fancy job in finance, an office in the World Trade Center. He was a man with a view of the world, and he was more than willing to share his wisdom.

Only Tony wasn't in the mood for a beer, wasn't in the mood for life lessons from an older brother. He was, in fact, in a funk—preoccupied with the direction of his life, with the prospect of law school, uncertain about all of it. That said, he sensed something in my father's voice. He said, "See you soon." Tony climbed into his brown Audi A4 and drove north, paralleling the Hudson River, a ten-minute drive. Not five. When he found the place, it was a dive, the name above the door painted in big black letters on something plastic and flimsy.

Tony walked into the bar, down a hallway to a separate room in the back. Dark and small, with a jukebox playing "Drops of Jupiter" by Train. At one end of the room, a pool table where John was playing with a couple of friends—Matt Sellitto, a Cantor Fitzgerald employee, and another man Tony didn't know, a cute brunette off to the side, the other guy's fiancée.

The other guy lived in Englewood, which explained how my father found the place.

The four men played pool, drank Rolling Rock, smoked cigars. Eventually, Tony asked why he was there. My father turned away from Sellitto and the other man, lowered his voice, said he was stressed. Said it as if confessing, like it was an admission of some kind. Said work was tough, and there was a new guy in the office he didn't like. He didn't hate the guy; he just didn't understand him. My father said he wanted to make a move. He wasn't happy. Life was too goddamn short to be unhappy.

Tony said, "Do it," the words coming so quickly sort of surprised him. Here he was a little brother offering advice to his big brother, and he kind of liked the feeling.

I was like the fourteen-year-old boy version of Nancy Drew. Here was my new plan. If, by sifting through photos and videos, I could identify specific clues—people, location, time of day, floor, which side of the building I was looking at, et cetera—I could then piece together the clues with my family's stories and eye witness accounts, and in a roundabout way, answer my question. So far I had: airplane crashes into building, phone call to mother, structure fills with smoke, second call to Uncle Tony, photo I hoped to find (with a small but visible timestamp in the lower corner) of a body (or body part) somewhere in the rubble or on the pavement. If I could do all that, I would then know with certainty how long he had suffered.

While working through my timeline scheme, I came across stories written by survivors—heroic tales about a work buddy or a Good Samaritan, a fireman or rescue worker, who saved a life and then died on the way out.

What I liked about these stories was the sense of closure. Even if these heroes didn't make it out, their families would know the truth, or at least a version of the truth far more palatable than the matter-of-fact language of an autopsy report. They would have a story with an ending to tell themselves and others.

After reading many such stories, and given that I knew my father as a selfless person, I believed I'd eventually come across a heroic story of his own. All I had to do was look. For two solid years, I came home from school each day and spent hours on my computer trying to locate one lousy story that included my father, one poorly written blog post, or an obscure online news article, even a reference in one of the many 9/11 memoirs popping up like pimples.

Did he jump or not? How long did he suffer? Was he a hero? Even if I had answers, I mean, goddamn double and triple fact-checked verifiable answers, would that be enough? Even if I had all the evidence in the world, would I come to terms with my father's death? Deep down, I don't think I would. But there was a chance, so I grabbed hold of a line of thinking—that knowing led to acceptance—that slowly dragged me down. I was quite frankly scared shitless of letting it go.

I started looking to my uncles for life advice, but also to ask questions about my dad. I was the oldest of four boys, and I had a whole bucket list of issues I couldn't discuss with my mom.

Uncle Sal, my mother's brother, was cool, a music lover. He had a bit of a temper, but it came off as funny to my brothers and me. We would all laugh at his sarcastic remarks or the way he would angrily drive. He'd take me with him skiing to Killington in Vermont and Hunter Mountain in upstate New York and Camelback in the Poconos. We went mountain biking in

Allamuchy Township and Lewis Morris Park. We even went to a few concerts together—McCartney and Kiss and Pearl Jam and Springsteen.

I could talk to Sal. I could talk to Uncle Tony, my father's brother, as well, but things were different between us. Tony was younger, late twenties. We played video games and did a lot of shouting at the big screen.

The older I got, the smarter I got, and the more pointed my questions. *What was my dad like as a man? What sort of things did you guys talk about?*

In theology class, one of the smarter kids, Chris, asked Ms. Robins if the people who jumped committed suicide. This was just weeks into my freshmen year at Seton Hall Preparatory School, a Roman Catholic all-boys' high school. Ms. Robins was nice, a genuinely kind woman. She thought about the question for a moment, then said, "They didn't go to work that day planning to jump."

"But they did," Chris argued.

"My point," she said. "They went to work like any other day. They were forced to jump or fall. Let's not forget some of them fell because of the horrible conditions inside the towers."

"What I'm asking...I mean, what I want to know is how God sees it?"

Ms. Robins was ready, had no doubt given this line of inquiry some forethought. She smiled. "On that day, they fell into the hands of God."

I liked the answer. It sounded, if not accurate, at least whimsical. By the end of the school day, however, I'd changed my mind. Her response came off as sort of preachy, even nonsensical. An hour later, I didn't know what I thought. I mean, I agreed the jumpers didn't commit suicide, if that's what she was saying. But I was still confused.

By the time I got home, I realized I had a bigger problem. I could easily talk to Sal and Tony about how funny and caring dad was. But I had no one to talk to, no one to ask, no one to set me straight on the sanctity of life because nobody wanted to be cross-examined about jumper intent or self-destruction or what God thought of the whole shebang. Why should they? By then, just a whiff of 9/11 in a question generated frowns, sometimes full-on migraines. And in a way, I'd made things worse by asking question after question. I was relentless. I was fourteen. My family could only endure so much. Sure, my fascination with jumpers and body parts and moral culpability was unproductive, even harmful to my ripening brain, but that didn't make it go away.

I don't remember exactly when, but at some point, all the adults in my life joined Mom and moved on. My mother and Sal and Tony and nearly every other adult I knew had had enough.

Everyone, that is, but Uncle Phil.

5

UNCLE PHIL WASN'T LIKE MY other uncles. He was an uncle by marriage, older—early-forties, thin hair, glasses. But none of that really described the man. If I had to choose a few words, I'd say funny, engaging, gray. By gray, I mean that no man's land between black and white—a mere blend of the two. Most of the adults in my life tended to be black and white. Good and bad. Right and wrong. Funny and flat-out inappropriate. With Phil, the boundaries were blurred or softened, or perhaps they didn't exist.

Oh, and he was fat. I didn't mention it because it feels irrelevant to even bring it up. But he was. I'm not good with estimates, but I'd say he was somewhat obese, two or even three of me.

The first week in September, Phil picked me up after school. This was my freshman year at the Prep—new school, new friends, new routines. Most days, I took the train to school and back home after soccer practice. I'd often get home after eight at night. I'd worked hard to make the soccer team as a freshman.

Seton Hall had one of the best soccer programs in the state. A year earlier, they'd won the Non-Public A, North Jersey Championship. Phil's construction company offices were in Maplewood, ten minutes away, maybe less, so every once in a while, he'd swing by and give me a lift home.

When Phil showed up, I didn't mind; in fact, I looked forward to it. I would get home earlier, but more importantly, while my mother and Uncle Sal and Uncle Tony had informally put the kibosh on any talk of 9/11, Phil did the opposite. He encouraged me to talk. He was open, likeable, had an expression about him that said, *Whatever's on your mind, out with it.*

When I was in eighth grade, he took me to Walmart to get a Valentine's Day gift for a girl I liked in class. As we were looking through the teddy bears and candy, he asked me if I ever fingered this girl. Next, he asked if I would let my friend jerk me off at a sleepover. Not things Sal or Tony would ask, but hell, I just went with it.

I spotted his big red Chevy Silverado truck in the upper parking lot, the name of his family's construction company painted on the door, and I climbed up into the passenger seat.

We drove up the hill adjacent to South Mountain Reservation, an enormous nature reserve I'd been to a few times. Northfield Avenue to Brookside Drive, sort of a shortcut across town.

Phil seemed nervous, accelerating fast and then braking too hard. He was acting strange, taking a bunch of quiet shallow breaths followed by a big nosy inhale. A bad day at work? Some irksome customer making demands? The thing was, Phil had a strange personality, so it was hard to tell strange from really strange.

We hadn't spoken three words.

One hand on the wheel, the other hand gripping his phone, he said, "A boy your age, you masturbate, right? Lotion, I'll bet you use lotion." He didn't look at me, just stared straight ahead. "When I was your age, geez, I can't even count the times I jerked off."

Phil had driven me home from school several times and sometimes grilled me about sex. Did I masturbate? Did I shave my pubic hair? Which direction? I remember him throwing out a hypothetical. *Say you woke in the middle of the night. Then you realized you weren't alone, a close friend was next to you, your penis in his hand, jerking you off. So, here's my question: Would you let him finish?*

I never answered, never needed to, because Phil would quickly start in with some new take on the facts of life. I saw it as trash talk, a grown-up letting his guard down, and except for the part about a friend with my dick in his hand, nothing more than the adult version of the shit-talking that went on in locker rooms or hallways or anywhere you allowed a bunch of naive, uninformed teenage boys to congregate.

Schoolwork and soccer drills and even uncles with spongy boundaries didn't bother me. What bothered me, or not bothered me exactly, what consumed me was my obsession with jumpers. I didn't think of it as an obsession, of course. I was curious. I liked to get to the bottom of things, and in the years since my father's death, I hadn't gotten anywhere near the bottom of anything. And in that moment, right then and there, a new kid in a new school—and by all outward appearances a kid who had everything going for him—I was a mess. When my brain had a spare millisecond, like in the truck with Phil, it turned on me. It took over and ran an unending series of images through my head, goddamn instant replay after instant replay, the same images I'd seen hundreds of times on the television and on my computer. Towers, smoke, jumpers. Fucking splat.

Not far from the house, I glanced at Phil, and then—sort of embarrassed at the words about to come out of me—I turned and faced out the truck's gargantuan windshield.

I asked, "Do you think my dad jumped?"

"Matt," he said, his tone ambivalent.

Phil could be hard to read, often impossible to interpret...say the way he pressed his lips tightly together, like now. Was that a smile or a grimace? Was he disappointed I asked? Was he half-ass saddened that in the last five years, I hadn't figured it out on my own? Or, like everyone else close to me, was he over it, and secretly wished I was too?

I said, "Do you? You can say if you do. Or don't. Or whatever."

"You have to understand, those people had no other way out."

"Wait. So you think it was his *only* way out?"

Phil flipped on his blinker and slowed, all his attention on the early evening traffic, and finally turned. "Not just your father, all of them, they made a choice."

"To jump, you're saying."

"Mmm."

"So you think he jumped?" I asked. "Or, wait, he *chose* to jump. My father chose to jump."

"I wasn't there. None of us were there."

"That's your answer—I wasn't there?"

He said, "You're upset."

"I don't know what you're saying."

"I think you do."

Here was the only relative in the bunch willing to face off, and he wouldn't even give me a straight answer.

I still had on my soccer outfit, white Adidas shorts, light grey shirt, Seton Hall Prep printed on the chest. My socks were pushed down to my ankles, showing off my skinny legs.

That's when he placed his phone on the big dashboard, leaned over and put his hand on my bare leg, the fingers up under my soccer shorts, and sort of moved his hand quickly upward. The man was grabbing my dick. Or was he? Maybe he was tickling me. Maybe he was...shit, I couldn't think what.

I pushed his hand away. I looked at him, straight at him, and waited for some explanation or excuse or whatever, and when none came, I laughed.

Ten minutes later, somewhere near Morristown, just past the Medical Center, Q104.3 blaring away on the radio, some pointless rock tune I couldn't get out of my head. Still driving, Phil reached over and grabbed my dick. His fat hand, strong and substantial, like a goddamn vise, gripping the nylon of my shorts and the flesh beneath.

My whole body tensed.

He said, "Hey, man, it's just us. You can relax."

I didn't speak.

His hand still on my dick, he squeezed and rubbed. He was gentle but not letting go. I shifted in my seat closer to the passenger door. I looked out the window. I was hot, flushed. And in short order, I got an erection. I looked at Phil, sweat on his fat forehead, a layer of oily moisture. And he stunk. Like a fat guy who'd been working outside in the heat all day.

I pushed his hand away. "Enough," I said.

"Matt, it's me here."

No response.

"You and me, we're just playing around. You know that, right? Right?"

Two weeks later, late September, we were driving in his car, a brand-new jet black BMW sedan. Once again, he asked me to masturbate with him.

I said, "No thank you." I didn't really say that. I can't remember precisely what I said, probably some impromptu mumbling, some exaggerated eye expression, lots of head shaking.

I want to point out to all you level-headed readers wondering why I didn't run for the hills, or why I didn't instantly shout for my mother, or even her new boyfriend, Joe, or later grab some official-looking adult, say a brawny school janitor or a teacher or even my coach, why I didn't do just about anything but what I did—which was sort of nothing—so here it is: I was fucking fourteen years old. And like I said, I was a mess.

I was school smart—not a straight-Aer, but close enough—and at the same time oblivious to the ways of the world. So when an otherwise swell person like my uncle Phil rattled off a bullet list of plausible reasons that an uncle and his young nephew should masturbate together—it's only natural, everyone's doing it, this is what uncles and nephews without a father do, he'd already masturbated with another uncle (not true, it turned out) so this is sort of a family tradition, and I didn't want to tarnish any family traditions, did I?—when an uncle makes his case with such clarity, such barefaced confidence, it's kind of hard for a kid to say no.

But I did. I said no.

Not now, not ever.

Now that the subject had been broached, however, Phil was relentless. Whenever we were alone, he'd tell me the invitation still stood.

No.

Suit yourself.

It was official. My uncle was gay, a flamer, a dicktickler, or one of the hundreds of other names the kids in school used. That meant something when it came to his marriage to my aunt, but what exactly, I had no clue. What did I care or even understand about the sexual shenanigans of grown men? What confused me was what he wanted to do with me. I was just his nephew and I knew I definitely wasn't gay.

I'd done my part. I'd said no. Several times.

And that was that.

Only it wasn't.

Later that month, things got way worse when I invited Phil to my house.

I'd spent the afternoon glaring at photos of jumpers on my computer. I'd scrolled through the images as fast as my little dumbass fingers would take me. Hundreds of the same photos, probably more. I stared at individual jumpers and couples and groups holding hands, all fleeing from the fire and smoke and eventually out into thin air where some amateur photographer caught them in the act.

I couldn't get enough.

Each new image took hold of me and kind of got in my head. Nevertheless, I needed to click on the next link, the next photo or video, and the next. Then I thought of my father, imagined him as a jumper. I imagined myself as a jumper, my whole body outside the tower, the momentary relief of not burning to death, then that rollercoaster downward pull, that pit-in-your-stomach feeling, and worst of all, being fully conscious just before hitting the ground.

I needed a break.

I typed in "Freedom Tower"—the early name for the main building of the rebuilt World Trade Center complex—and I sifted through computer-generated illustrations of the building design. A kind of "classical obelisk," some critic called it. Once complete, it'd be the tallest building in the Western Hemisphere, the sixth tallest in the world. Construction of the footings and foundations had started just months earlier in April.

As I swiped through Google images, I stumbled upon a graphic picture of a jumper's remains. One I hadn't seen before. Nothing was left of the person, just a mass of red goo. For some reason, this particular photograph stunned me.

Maybe I was extra emotional that day. Maybe I needed a good cry. Maybe my brain chemistry was playing tricks on me. I mean, by now, I could look at anything. I was normally as hardened to blood and guts as a grizzled M.E., which was how I pictured a medical examiner—white-haired and grizzled.

I needed to talk to someone.

Lo and behold, the only person who would talk to me about such things was Uncle Phil.

I grabbed my cell phone and punched in his number. "It's me, Matt," I said, my voice crackly.

"What's up, Meatball?"

I fucking hated that nickname. "I just looked at some pictures on the Internet." I sobbed into the phone.

"Injured people, you mean?"

"Sort of."

"People who jumped?"

More sobbing.

"I'm sorry you saw that. Give me the web address. I want to see what you saw."

I rattled off the URL.

I don't recall what we said then, but an hour later, he showed up at my house. He let himself in and walked upstairs to my bedroom, the door closed behind him. Phil leaned against the doorframe like a man without a care in the world.

He said, "What are you looking at?"

"You know," I said. I showed him a video I'd just watched a dozen times.

I'd put the question to Phil again. "Was my father a jumper?"

This time, he answered. No vacillating, no awkward pauses. "Yes," he said.

And for the first time, Uncle Dickweasel sort of made sense. My dad worked way up in the towers, no way out, the conditions unbearable, so he jumped. Fine. Now I knew.

My computer was set up next to the bed so I could sit on the bed and surf away. Phil sat on the bed next to me. He pulled the little desk that held my computer closer.

He reached up and typed on my keyboard. A website opened with a bunch of little boxes, each box a video. All the boxes showing off naked people. Porn. He clicked on one of the boxes, the one with a young kid and an older woman.

"What are you looking for?" I asked.

"This isn't a search. Look for yourself."

"I mean, this is my computer."

"Come on, bud. I told you, it's what uncles and nephews do together. Don't worry about it."

I peeked at the open door. No one else was home.

Phil said, "What are you worried about?"

I wasn't worried. I was confused, closer to discombobulated, a word I'd never said aloud in my life. "Nothing, I guess."

"Do you think I would hurt you?"

Now I was worried. "No. I just don't understand why you're showing me that," I said, pointing at my iMac.

Phil thought for a moment, turned his head to the door, said, "Let me see your penis."

"What? No."

"Come on. Just take it out for a second." He looked around my room, stopped at a photo of my brothers and my mom on my desk. He said, "Your mom said we should have a little talk—the birds and bees." It was the kind of thing my mother would do, have one of my uncles give me the straight scoop about sex, and for the first time in a while, I believed him.

If my mom trusted Phil, why shouldn't I?

He reached up, took my mouse, and clicked on another video. "You gotta see this." We both watched a young boy and girl crawl into bed. "Come on," he said. "Let me see it."

I still wore my school clothes, shirt, tie, and khakis.

Something about it still didn't sit right with me. But, well... fuck it. I pulled my pants down.

He did the same and we wacked off and watched porn.

So there we were, just an uncle and his young nephew lying mostly naked on my bed watching a lady with big tits and this skinny dude fucking. When Phil finished, he toweled off the whitish goo from his stomach with one of my dirty soccer socks, pulled on his work jeans and tucked in his shirt. "Okay," he said. "I think we're good."

As crazy as it sounds, I thought of my father, the courage it took to jump, what he looked like after he landed.

We had several conversations around this time—September, October, November 2006—and a few text exchanges. One time we got into a conversation about my mother.

Phil said, "Your mom didn't wait that long after your dad died to be with someone else." He waited for a reaction. "Romantically," he added. "You know what I'm saying?"

Mom met Joe back in August 2006. Joe was compact; I imagined as a young guy, he was a fighter. From a distance, he was quiet, a man who kept to himself. Up close...well, I wouldn't know because I never got that close.

"What are you talking about?" I asked.

"She was with a couple guys. Not long after 9/11."

I said nothing. I felt like I had been told a devastating truth, like Santa isn't real.

"And, you know Joe. Just look at him."

"Look at him?" I asked.

Phil tilted his head, his way of rolling his eyes, as if to say, *Come on, man. We're buds. You know what I'm talking about*, which, of course, I didn't. He said, "Okay, fine, I'll say it. Joe cheats on your mom."

"Cheats on her?"

"You didn't know?"

I shook my head.

"You know the type. Did it before they married. Nothing's changed since."

"I'm not sure I believe.... Well, I'm not saying you're lying, but—"

He cut me off. "Look, I had a buddy do some looking around, not a full investigation, you understand. This was before they got married. For your mom's own good. I don't want to come between you and your stepdad, but Joe was seen with another woman not a week before the wedding."

"Wait, what?" I said.

Here came the punch line.

"It's hard to know who to trust," he said. "Don't worry, kid, you got me. That's all that matters."

6

In October, things got worse. I was at a sleepover at Uncle Phil's, there for my cousins little Tess, Scotty, and Isaak. When everyone went to bed, Phil scooted me away to his office, shut the door, and pulled up some porn on his computer. I stood there with a sense of hesitation. He rubbed his hand over my penis from the outside of my pants, which I quickly pulled away from.

"Let's go in the basement," he said.

"No, I really want to go to bed."

Conveniently for him, the door to the basement could only be accessed from his office. He opened the door slowly, told me to go down first. Each step made a creepy creaking sound as I descended into the basement. One small light hanging from the ceiling barely lit up the room. There were boxes and boxes of crap everywhere, chairs and old storage stuff piled up, all enclosing on one chair with the light directly above. He clearly planned on bringing me, or someone else down here. Were there others before me?

He came downstairs and told me to sit on the chair. My legs were restless, twitching constantly. There wasn't a sound to be heard, and I knew that if I were to scream, no one would hear me. Or would they? I wanted to scream up to my aunt, but the words wouldn't come out of my mouth. It was as if my mouth was sewn shut.

"Please, Uncle Phil, I just want to go to bed."

"What are you so scared of, Matt? It's just me."

"I know, but I just feel uncomfortable is all."

"There's nothing to worry about."

But I still couldn't help but be worried.

He told me to take my pants off, and I did. He bent down and started masturbating me. I looked up at the small light bulb hanging from the ceiling—the light seemed so bright, as if a floodlight was shining in my face. I tried to force myself to ejaculate just so I could get the whole thing over with. I closed my eyes, and I did.

After I finished, he told me I could go to bed. I felt so weak and dirty, I ran up the stairs to bed, hoping to forget the whole event ever occurred.

He stayed down in the basement long after I left. I heard him come up the stairs, and he opened the door to the guest room I was staying in. Was he going to make me do something to him now?

I faced the wall away from the door, pretending to be asleep. "Are you awake?" he whispered into the room.

I tried not to make a sound, holding back inevitable tears that seemed impossible to hold in any longer. I didn't answer, and he closed the door slowly.

I wanted to tell my mom, someone, what happened. But couldn't manage to fight my way out of the psychological maze that I seemingly put myself in. I quietly cried myself to sleep that night.

Roughly a month later, the whole family was at Grandma Laura's over in Florham Park. Sunday dinner. Big gathering.

Maggie, Phil's wife, needed more pasta. "Run home," she said to him. "Grab the penne. It's way back in the top cabinet. Go."

The guy's fat face actually lit up. I was in the hall, and on his way out, he said, "Come with me on an errand for your aunt Maggie."

"I don't know."

He grabbed an old work coat and moved to the door. "She's waiting."

One of my cousins, Scotty, asked to come along.

"I need to talk to Matt. Another time, buddy."

Phil and Maggie lived just down the street and around the corner on Hanover Road. Ten minutes round-trip, tops. We got to Phil's house, and he parked his truck in the driveway. I said, "I'll wait."

"Nonsense. I want to show you something."

I didn't want to go in the house, but I also didn't want to say no. I was the good kid, the one who tried to get along, the one who never said no. I was worried, I suppose, what might happen if I did say no. I followed him inside, and then upstairs and into his bedroom, where he rooted around in his closet and finally surfaced with a DVD case, black and scuffed, no writing on it. Recorded porn. He slipped the DVD into the player and waited for it to load. A menu came up.

"Pick something," he said. "I'll get the pasta."

"I'll wait."

"What are you afraid of? Pick something."

I shrugged.

"Pick something." He wriggled his eyebrows in a way meant to be funny. "If you don't, I will."

I knew what he meant. He liked big tits, some girl on girl, but mostly tits.

He ran down the stairs, made some noise in the kitchen, and ran back up the stairs. He breathed hard, sweated. As I said, my uncle was fat, not made for stairs. He stopped to catch his breath, then moved to the window and pulled down the blinds. He stood there, peeking through a slit in the blinds, checking out the neighbors, the street, I didn't know what. He stood back from the window, paused, and then took another peek.

"What?" I asked.

"It's nothing."

"What?"

"You didn't tell anyone?"

"Tell them what?"

"Nothing. Nothing. It's nothing. I got the pasta. I can't forget the pasta."

I didn't feel good. "I've got to use the bathroom."

When I returned, my uncle Phil was sprawled naked on the bed, his massive gut like an elephant on its back. His khaki pants and gray-white underwear on the floor. I smelled sweat.

He patted the bed beside him and told me to take my pants off.

"Please, let's just go back. Aunt Maggie and my mom will get weirded out if we take a while."

"Don't worry, they trust you with me."

He got down on his knees, and I could feel a chill slowly going down my spine. My whole body locked up, and I instantly felt as if a shell of cool, brisk air was overflowing me. I tried closing my eyes, thinking of a better place, thinking of my dad saving me. Surely, someone would get suspicious and come to my rescue. He pulled my pants down to my ankles, goosebumps traveling up my legs towards my penis.

"I'll go nice and slow, just relax," he said, grinning from ear to ear.

I felt his calloused hands grab my penis, and slowly, I got an erection. I opened my eyes, made eye contact with him. He could see I was trying to get up and pushed me back down quickly before I could say a word. I could feel my body tense up.

He started sucking my dick. I could see him rubbing his penis while he performed oral sex on me.

"What are you doing?" I asked.

"Relax, Meatball. Doesn't it feel good?"

As fucked up as this whole situation was, it did feel good. But I didn't want him to make me feel this good. I wanted to cry. I wanted to punch him in the face. I wanted to run away and never look back. I closed my eyes and thought of a pretty girl, and voila, it was over.

"Now, it's my turn," he said.

"What? No."

"Hey, fair's fair."

"Sorry, but I'm not going to," I said.

He was red in the face, out of breath or angry, I didn't know which. "I did you, now you do me."

"This is weird," I said. "Mom would think it's weird. Aunt Maggie."

"You tell anyone about this, they'll think you're gay. You want that? Your mom, Maggie, they wouldn't understand, trust me. It's a guy thing."

"Shit." I put his dick in my mouth, held it there for about five seconds and stopped. "I can't do it."

"Rub my balls."

I rubbed and squeezed and when he finished, he rolled out of bed, almost crushing me in the process, and walked into the bathroom. I felt like a dirty dishrag, little dumbass tears running down my face.

Right before my dad died, he got me the children's version of the book *PT-109*, and he got the adult version for himself. He made sure that I read it during the summer of 2001 before I went back to school, no telling why. The book chronicles JFK's life in the Navy, how he and the PT-109 successfully evacuated Marines while dodging Japanese mortars when the boat ran out of fuel. We didn't talk about the book, but I knew his giving it to me was my dad's way of telling me, "This is what courage and strength looks like Matt. And this is what is important for a man to possess, courage and strength."

I lost myself that day. I lost my innocence, and any remaining hopes of what was left in order to have a relatively normal adolescence. Courage and strength? I didn't have a clue.

I got a long seven-month break. In June, just after my fifteenth birthday, Phil cornered me again. We were down the shore in Long Beach Island—LBI to the locals—a barrier island in Ocean County, New Jersey. White sandy beaches, lots of restaurants, a lighthouse, a regular tourist haven. We rented a place big enough for a bunch of my family—Mom and Joe, his kids Michael and Brittany; my brothers little Paul, Michael, Nicholas; Phil and Maggie and their kids, little Tess, Scotty, Isaak, and Liz. Even my grandparents Sal and Laura stayed for a night or two. Some of Joe's family stopped by. The place was a zoo. A bunch of us kids and Phil were rinsing off sand in the outdoor shower. Everyone scrambled away, and I stood there with Phil in his bathing suit and his fat gut, and a moment later, his suit was down around his fat feet. He took my hand and put it on his dick, and I tugged and pulled until he got jizz everywhere. Then he got on his knees and gave me a blowie.

I masturbated him. He performed oral sex on me.

It sounds cold because that's how I thought of it. One, two, we're done. I tried to make it go by as quickly as possible and keep face and pretend nothing was wrong. Deep down, I found it so odd that my uncle was so willing to risk his marriage for some sort of perverted version of being a father figure.

Months went by and I hadn't heard much from him. In December, he texted me a bunch, mostly inviting me to get together and watch a movie, code for cozy up to a computer screen of porn. I declined.

The following June, I tromped off once again to LBI with Phil and his family, along with their friends Ken and Francene— in an attempt to avoid vacation with my mom, brothers, and Joe. By this time, it had been almost a year since anything had happened with Phil. I thought, maybe things would be different this time, especially with their family friends there. I was wrong, of course. Francene was beautiful, in her forties, luscious brown hair flowing past her shoulders—and I had a crush on her, as most teenage boys would. When my uncle Phil found that out, he used his mind tricks to have his way with me one final time.

I made a vow to myself then to never let it happen again—if he tried again, I would fight him off somehow and not give in anymore.

Months later, he caught me in the garage at my house. Just the two of us. He said, "Matt, it's been so long since we hung out."

"I've been busy. You know."

"Come on. Why haven't we gotten together?"

"Uncle Phil, I don't want to."

He paused, thinking of a way to turn things around, the fraud. "That hurts my feelings. I mean it, it does. What we have, it's...well, unique."

"I'm not doing it again."

"Matt..."

"Not ever."

By then, I was sixteen. I'd had enough.

Here was the big question: Now what?

I wanted to tell my mom, but I was afraid. There was no telling what she'd do, no telling the reaction I'd get from my brothers or my friends at Seton Hall Prep. The rabbit hole I jumped into when I began my obsession to figure out how my father died was darker and wider, and since I couldn't see a way out, I crawled in deeper.

More questions. How did I allow this thing with Uncle Phil to happen? Did this make me gay? I knew I wasn't attracted to men, but my actions made me think otherwise. I was so confused, not knowing what to think or who to talk to. Sometimes when I felt the moment was just right to tell someone, I would fight to force the words out of my mouth, to the point that they'd reach the tip of my tongue, almost begging to be spit out—then I'd swallow them back into my empty being. The mental torment sexual abuse inflicts on a child can sometimes be worse than the abuse itself. When it comes at the hands of a family member, it makes it much harder to come forward. And that's what happened to me. The shame and guilt would corrode my mind for a long time. Was this all my fault? All I wanted to do was pretend that none of this happened.

So I said nothing.

By this time, I was smoking weed. Puff, inhale, forget it ever happened. I tried to pretend as if I was just another kid at school, one with a normal family and life. One who didn't have an uncle that fiddled with him.

I stayed clear of Phil, and I ignored his text messages. At family gatherings, of which we had many, I walked on eggshells. If Phil was in one room, I'd meander to another. If I had to take out the trash, I'd make sure he was way at the other end of the house, and then grab the trash and sprint to the garage and back. No way he'd have time to catch me alone. At the dinner table, I did my best to sit at the opposite end of the table. I tried to keep conversations normal in front of other people, with a smiley façade. I didn't want anyone to question why I wanted to be as far away from him as possible. On the few occasions I sat across from him, I made it seem like nothing ever happened. I tried to keep my head down—my plan to avoid some daffy wink or pigheaded innuendo tossed my way—wolfed down my meal, and said I had to go meet a friend or I had to use the bathroom, whatever I thought would get me out of there pronto.

The crazy thing is, for a while, I pretended that things were normal. I would talk to Phil about other things, like sports. You see, Phil was the cool uncle—the cool family member for that matter. Everyone liked and trusted him, so me disrupting the family peace with an atomic bomb didn't seem like a good idea. I thought, if he would act like it never happened, then maybe I could too. Maybe I could live a normal life and not have night-mares all the time. That obviously wasn't the case.

He'd sometimes text his favorite line: *We need to get together, watch a movie.*

No.

It's just you and me.

Stop texting me.

Uncle Phil had told me my father jumped. Closure. Peace of mind, right? So why had it led me down this hellhole of a rela-tionship with this horrible guy? I was almost a grown-up now, and it was seven years since 9/11. My mother along with her new husband—whose faithfulness or lack thereof I was never able to confirm—had checked out of the past. It was time for me to be a role model for Nick, Mike, and Paul. I wanted to be a goddamn pillar of strength, a regular JFK—hell, a regular JPB, the man of the house. I wanted to protect my mom and my brothers. And I had failed. My soccer coach had said my dad would have been proud of me. Proud? My own fall was just beginning.

7

VILLANOVA, A PRIVATE SCHOOL IN the Philadelphia suburbs, was my first choice for college. Hard to say why I wanted to go to Villanova—perhaps a #1 ranking by *U.S. News & World Report*, phenomenal basketball program, outstanding academics, welcoming atmosphere, woodsy campus. Could be because one of my best friends from Seton Hall Prep, Blake, wanted to follow in his father's footsteps and attend the school. His enthusiasm was infectious. So I took the SAT—scored a disappointing average—worked extra hard to compensate with good grades, and sent in my application. The acceptance letter arrived, the paper stiff and creamy yellow, with an official seal at the top. On the surface, life was good and was heading to even better. My best friend from elementary school, Fitzy, also got accepted to Villanova, and we planned to room together.

I'd developed some lousy habits in the last couple of years at Seton Hall Prep. While I was good at school and sports, I was exceptionally good at drinking and smoking pot. I was so good,

I'd often smoke throughout the week, occasionally get screw-ball-loopy on the weekends, and still bring home stellar grades. I had it all under control.

Just before the end of high school, Fitzy and Blake and I road-tripped down to Villanova to visit a friend. Will was in a fraternity, Phi Gamma Delta, nicknamed Fiji, known as a heavy party fraternity on campus and often in hot water with the university. Will showed us a good time, impossible not to, really, dragging us off campus to one unruly party after another. After a single night, I was sold on rushing Fiji my freshman year.

Late nights pledging and early morning classes; it was impossible to do both, at least for me, without some sort of substance, a little pick me up at the right time. Someone handed me an Adderall before going to study, used to treat attention deficit hyperactivity disorder. For years as a kid, I evaded being medicated with stimulants like my brothers or any other young kid with ADHD. But the moment I swallowed that pill, that was it. I felt elated—a seemingly eternal smile across my face. In that moment I knew there was no turning back. Forget balance, and instead, wash down a little pale-orange 30 milligram pill, a combination of amphetamine and dextroamphetamine, a couple of mega stimulants, wait twenty minutes, and get ready for an extra shot of impulse control.

When it came to homework, Adderall was the drug of choice. Cramming for a test? Pop a pill and you were good to go. Even before my first class, I'd swallow a half, then put in a full day of classes, down another half to quiet myself enough for three or four hours of uninterrupted homework, and maybe gobble up another half for the night ahead and whatever the house had in store for us pledges.

The first time I tried Adderall, I texted my buddy, my supplier.

Dude, this shit is awesome.

Who is this?

Funny. It's like a magic pill. Everyone should take this shit.

It's college. Everyone does.

Freshman year at Villanova was a blast. What I remember of it.

At the end of the school year, maybe late May, I was back home in New Vernon and had been referred to a neurologist over in Berkeley Heights, a young guy, narrow-faced, glasses too big for his head, and I asked about Adderall. Buying the drug on campus was batshit crazy expensive. I needed my own supplier, or at least someone to help cover the cost. Enter my friends at Horizon Blue Cross Blue Shield of New Jersey. I said all the right things, he diagnosed me with ADHD, and I was golden. Now, I just needed the right treatment.

"What about it?" the neurologist inquired.

"Some kids at school told me about it."

"You've tried it?"

"No, I mean, maybe once. I couldn't focus, so I asked a friend..."

"Did your *friend* tell you about the side effects?"

When he said friend, I heard your *fucking friend* or your *fake friend*, his way of suggesting, *why don't you stop screwing around with me, kid.* This was a side of him I'd never seen before.

I shook my head. Real puppy-dog-like.

"This *friend* of yours, he prescribed a Schedule II controlled substance without giving you all the information." He turned away and started typing on a keyboard. "Rapid or irregular heartbeat, delirium, panic, psychosis, heart failure. These are the most common side effects. Could be others."

"Oh," I said.

"Did he tell you not to use Adderall if you have glaucoma, an overactive thyroid, severe agitation, high blood pressure? A bad heart?" Here the man stopped and glared at me, said, "A history of drug or alcohol addiction?"

"No," I said.

I was playing along. None of that stuff mattered—what mattered was homework with Adderall or homework without it, and by now, I wasn't even sure I could do homework without it. I thought to myself, can students in top universities really do homework without cognitive-enhancing drugs, and if so, why?

He scooted his little stool closer to me. "I want you to try a couple of other medications first."

"Of course," I said, and then I tried the other meds. Two weeks later, told him they didn't do a thing for me, and I got my cherished Adderall.

Syllabus week, the way it was explained to me, was a Greek tradition in which the individual mission was to drink and party every night for a week straight, sleep late in the morning, and not attend a single class.

I could do that.

Sophomore year, first week of classes.

Here we go. Night one went off without a hitch.

Night two, I got blackout drunk. At some point—it's hard to put my finger on—I started throwing up. Hunched over, moving slowly forward, getting hours-old penne pasta and spicy red sauce on a new two-hundred-dollar pair of 7 For All Mankind jeans and equally pricey Clarks Wallabee boots—sort of upscale moccasins, maple suede, a color impossible to get clean once you've treated them to a night of puking. I was staring at my shoes when I walked face-first into a car.

My memory is foggy here, but I do recall lying on the ground and staring up into the mug of an EMT, black tee-shirt, gray button-down with patches. He tells me they're taking me to Bryn Mawr Hospital.

"What for?" I asked.

"Apparently, your first VEMS ride."

VEMS stood for "Villanova Emergency Medical Service," a student-run, volunteer ambulance service. VEMS was called when a student was so drunk he needed a lift to the hospital, where he—me—would get my stomach pumped, poked with an IV and filled with fluids, and invited (ordered) to stay the night, or as long as it took to sober up and walk out the door on my own. When I woke up, I called a frat buddy who drove over, picked me up, and carted me back to campus.

I moved slowly. My head hurt. I couldn't think. When we stopped in front of my dorm, Sullivan Hall, I yanked on the door handle, which slipped out of my hand. Tried again, another slip. My buddy finally reached over and opened my door.

He said, "Out you go."

"I still can't remember what happened."

"Man, you look bad."

"How bad?"

"Your skin, it's like...I don't know, fishy, I guess. Get some sleep. We got a big night ahead."

"Okay. I'll see you tonight."

School was tough for me. Adderall prescription aside, I still found it hard to truly concentrate in class. Homework and studying for tests were a whole different beast—a multitude of YouTube tabs sprinkled across my screen at all times. I began contemplating it all: which major to declare, who I truly wanted to be, or if I even possessed the skills necessary to succeed in life.

Maybe this was all an excuse so I didn't have to do the work. I don't know, but none of it made sense to me. I was miserable. I started wondering if I really wanted to be in the business school after all. I reached out to Uncle Tony for advice or guidance or whatever. Someone who would give me advice my dad would give. Someone who sounded like him, too.

"Yo, what's up?" he said, picking up on the first ring.

"Not much, dude. I wanted to talk about school. I don't know if you're free...?"

He could sense the panic in my voice. I came off as frantic, almost wanting to rush the conversation.

"What's wrong? Everything okay?"

"I'm thinking about dropping out of the business school and switching to the Liberal Arts school."

"Why?" He paused and took a deep breath. "I am telling you right now, that this will be a decision you will regret. Think of your résumé. Villanova's business school is one of the best."

"I know, I know. The work is just so hard. I can't do it, dude. I really can't."

"I get that," he said, a nurturing, father-like tone to his voice, "but look. I am going to tell you stick with it. Your dad would say the same thing if he was here."

Did I really want to be in finance? Did I want to work a job I hated every day for the rest of my life, just like my dad—a job he was going to quit, but got killed for instead? At the end of the day, it didn't matter what was best for me. I had made up my mind and officially dropped out of the business school.

Months later, I flew home for Christmas break and spent days in the house all by myself. My brothers were still in school, and my mom was out doing her Christmas shopping. I wandered from room to room. One day I ended up in my father's office where I thumbed through books on the shelf, many my mother had picked up over the years about the World Trade Center attacks. I pulled on the closet door. It was locked. I was curious, so I tried to pick the lock with a paperclip to no avail. I searched the office and found the hidden keys to the closet in one of the desk drawers. I opened the closet, and there was tons of shit in there. Big metal storage drawers filled with paperwork and bills, old printers and fax machines, and a big, brown unmarked box way in the back.

I opened the box, and it contained countless 9/11 artifacts. I dug through some old newspaper articles, flyers, emails, letters, and more stuff, all of it apparently gathered up and organized and put away for safekeeping by my mother. All of the newspaper articles mentioned my dad and described my family in detail. There were tons of envelopes labeled "The Bocchi Boys Fund," presumably in which people sent money to us out of sympathy or something.

I found a missing persons flyer of my dad near the top of the box. *If you have seen or heard from John or know any information please contact....* In the center of the flyer was a picture of my dad, crouched down in front of his Porsche, smiling. I started to cry, thinking how absurd the whole situation was, how my dad went to work like any normal day and was murdered. Then my family put together these missing persons flyers as if he was kidnapped or something. I imagined hundreds or thousands of these flyers posted up all over lower Manhattan.

Near the bottom of the box, I found a thick manila envelope with a government seal on the front and a string to keep the contents from spilling out of the back. Inside was a plastic baggy, and inside the baggy was my father's wallet, money clip, several credit cards bound together by a rubber band, a single business card, a gym membership card to The Fitness Company, and a fifteen-year-old key to his Porsche.

The wallet was waterlogged and burned, the brown leather moldy in the center, and charred along one edge.

I'd never seen any of this.

The box, the manila envelope, the personal items. None of it.

The paper clip caught my eye because it held a bunch of twenty-dollar bills no one apparently felt like spending, and directly beneath the rusted clip was a photo of me and Nick and Mike, my face barely visible from the water damage to the photo.

Also in the manila envelope was a sheaf of loose papers from the City of New York. On top was a Certificate of Death, a document I didn't know existed.

I scanned the cert:

DEATH WAS CAUSED BY: (A) Immediate Cause— Multiple Blunt Trauma.

Certifier Signature: Dr. Milewski

I later learned that the overwhelming majority of remains were so difficult to identify the New York Medical Examiner listed all of the deaths at the World Trade Center that day as "homicide due to blunt force trauma." This included those who died in the collapse of the towers, as well as the poor souls who fell or jumped.

In another document, I saw a sketch depicting which parts they found of my dad—tiny Xs scattered across a stick figure body. The medical examiner had called my mother after 9/11—a favor provided by a neighbor of ours—and was told that due to the low amount of blood in my father's muscle tissue, evidence indicated he was most likely in the building's stairwell when it collapsed. His death was quick, and he didn't suffer. "Alive one minute, gone the next," as the M.E. had brashly put it.

My father was *not* a jumper.

But I was never told.

Suddenly it all hit me. I realized what Phil had been doing all along. He lied to me. Not to save me from future dead-end research that would cause me to continue to spiral deeper and deeper into this hole. Not to prevent me from looking at the same pictures and videos of jumpers over and over and over again. But so that I would do whatever he wanted, like a fucking puppet. He had me under his thumb the entire time, and I was too stupid to realize it.

And worst of all, my mother knew I was obsessed with my father's cause of death, but still, she never told me the full truth. I mean, she briefly mentioned the phone call from the M.E. around this time, but it had a hush-hush feel to it and almost came across as insignificant. Sort of like school gossip you hear in the hallways. Still, it took confronting her about the box remnants to get the details that could truly help me piece the puzzle together. Was she trying to spare me pain? Or could she not even think about the truth herself, much less share it with someone else? When I found the box, I didn't think about her reasons for not telling me. I was just pissed.

Rather than solve a long-standing mystery—was my father a jumper?—the contents of the box confirmed something I'd long suspected: that more information about 9/11 existed. I just never thought I'd find it in my own house. And if it existed, then my somewhat fading obsession with the events of that day had new legs. There must be, I thought, even more facts and evidence and first-hand narratives—in closets and basements, on computer drives, in some reluctant old codger's head—and if the goods existed, I could, given time and a good measure of luck, find them. If my mother could squirrel away information from her own sons for the past ten years, why not other mothers and fathers trying to protect their own little ones or other family members or even friends, by withholding reports and documents and personal items and who knows what?

The craziest aspect of the official-looking manila envelope: it gave me hope. If I could keep the faith, if I could stay on point, I would someday cobble together more than just a timeline. I'd find a narrative, a story, not my mother's or Tony's or mine, but my father's.

But first there was spring semester to think about, and I started it with a clear goal: consume as many pills as possible. Enough with Adderall...I was eager to move on to painkillers. A pledge brother, Travis, snatched up a bunch of oxycodone, 30 milligram pills, nicknamed "blues" for their light blue tint. He bought them from a kid in The Exchange, a hip café on campus intended for students to do homework and eat, but would do for the occasional drug drop.

I lived just off N Ithan Avenue in one of the larger residence halls, and a stone's throw from the School of Business and the University Counseling Center. Chester and Jones lived down the hall. We were playing a video game in their room, *FIFA 12*, when

Travis arrived. He held up a small plastic bag with a handful of baby-blue pills inside. "Look what I got."

"About time," I said. I had butterflies. I was ready.

"You ever done blues? Shit feels like you're stoned, but better."

I was gripped with excitement, even as a flurry of nervousness swept through my body. I grabbed a twenty-dollar bill from my wallet. Then a debit card. I took one of the pills and put it on the desk, laid the bill over the pill, and the hard plastic card over the bill, and I pressed down hard with my arms. Crunch. I felt the pill give into itself and flatten on the desk top. I flipped the card over and pressed, this time with the little raised edges of my name on the card grinding into the powder. I didn't want any chunks. Chester or Jones, I can't recall which, was doing the same.

A race.

I moved the card in a circular motion, making the circle of blue powder even bigger. I used the edge of the card to chop the powder into a fine dust, parted the dust into a line, and used the rolled twenty like a straw to inhale the dust up my right nostril.

I win.

The dust bunched somewhere deep in my nasal cavity and then dripped slowly down the back of my throat. My first impulse was to gag.

I sat down on the futon and waited for the fireworks.

Ten minutes later I felt dreamy, floaty, an ooze flowing through my body like cuddly little worms. Then a wave of warmth came over me, a fuzzy-blanket kind of feel. All my cares disappeared. I didn't think of my dad or 9/11 or how he died or how long he suffered. That feeling of uselessness and that shell of coldness I felt after being sexually abused, well, I had the exact opposite feeling in this moment. I felt warm and happy and invincible. The only narrative that I cared about was the happiness-soaked one of the now. Nothing else mattered. If I thought ahead at all it was to plan my next high, to give myself a shot at feeling this way forever.

The next day, I tried another painkiller and fell in love.

And my lover was Actavis Pharma, the maker of generic oxycodone.

One night my girlfriend, Sofia, called and said she was going out with her girlfriends.

"We have a thing at the house," I said. "I told you about it days ago. It's like in a couple of hours. Less, I guess."

"A party?"

"Not just a party," I said.

"Well, I've got this other thing, is all."

I was furious. She always had an excuse for everything. Normally, I knew how to pace myself, say 45 or even 60 milligrams of oxycodone a day should keep the works appropriately oiled. I sold blues on campus by this time and therefore had a regular supply of the pills flowing through my fingers, which made it all the harder to keep track of how many went up my nose. Sometimes my timing was off, and I'd do pills on top of pills. I'd show her, I thought, so I snorted a big bullet of oxy, 45 milligrams, maybe more, it was hard to tell sometimes. I gave it a couple of minutes to kick in, then took the stairs down and outside for a smoke. When I got outside, so high I was bleary-eyed, there she was, Sofia in the flesh, massive smile, knockout figure. Puerto Rican. Hot-tempered.

"Surprise," she said.

"It's you."

Lame reaction. She could tell something was wrong. Eventually, I fessed up to the oxy, which didn't go over well. She shouted. I was still dopey, euphoric, in no mood for a meaningful give-and-take and that made her sullen, and then irate. Before I could turn the ship around, she broke up with me.

"You want some advice?" she asked. Off my look she said, "Want it or not, you need to stop. The pills, drinking, it's out of hand. Tell me you can see that."

"Okay, okay. I'll stop. I promise. I mean, I really promise." I think I was slurring my words when I said it.

"You're pathetic."

I could get another girlfriend.

I couldn't get enough pills.

Me, oxy, Opana, and a bunch of others were like *this*—imagine my pointer and middle finger crossed—throughout January and February and the first week of March. The next week, spring break 2012, I flew down to the Bahamas for what amounted to Villanova Greek Week. On the flight, my high wore painfully thin. Well before we landed, my body revolted. Hot sweats followed by cold sweats. Goosebumps. Aches all over.

We touched down in Nassau and checked into a dumpy hotel.

By then, I felt nine steps past miserable. It'd been about fourteen hours since I put anything useful up my nose. I'd never experienced withdrawal. Why would I? The smart play was to keep myself medicated. Forever. Only I didn't bring any pills with me, an effort to tell myself I wasn't addicted to painkillers. An hour later, I had the shakes. I grabbed my laptop and looked up oxycodone withdrawal. Yikes, I had all the earmarks—sweating, goosebumps, vomiting, anxiety, insomnia, and muscle pain.

I sat on the bed, with a wavy aqua-blue bedspread and coral-colored pillows meant to make me think scuba diving and snorkeling, but it didn't work. Instead, I thought of what it would feel like once I got my hands on some little blue pills or some greens or pinks. Something I could snort to take away this feeling. Once my ass hit the bed, something inside me gurgled and only got louder. I ran to the bathroom. First, to shit my brains out. Next, to throw up everything in my stomach until I tasted bile. Wait sixty seconds. Rush to the bathroom. Repeat.

Only two things could break the cycle: another pill (which I didn't have) or time.

Waiting out withdrawal, at least from what I'd seen in movies, was just awful, and I was an hour past awful. Worse, withdrawal on a spring break trip sucked because I didn't have the ambition to drink. Just the thought of a Bahama Mama or a Pineapple Upside-Down Martini made me gag.

I tried snorting some cocaine, hoping that getting high on some other drug would make me forget I was in opiate withdrawal. Or forget that I had been doing enough oxy to put me into withdrawal in the first place. Maybe I thought it would allow me to feel like every other person on spring break. Doing coke and binge drinking all day. "Normal," so to speak.

The high only lasted a few minutes. All it really did was make me jittery and want to throw up more.

Soon my roommates, Schneider and Johnson, a couple of oxy-heads like me, were determined to find some painkillers—Percocet, Vicodin, OxyContin. Anything. Schneider said he sort of felt weird. Maybe he was experiencing withdrawal too. Johnson called around until he found a friend from Villanova with some Percocet. Fifteen minutes later, he stood next to the bed.

"How do we do this?" I asked.

"Parachute," Johnson said.

"You sure?"

Johnson nodded, with a sly grin on his face.

"What do you have?" I asked. "Two point fives. Five milligrams?"

"Ten milligrams."

I smiled.

Since Percocet pills included acetaminophen, not to mention they were coated with who knows what, they were no good to snort—too painful, and would only screw up an otherwise good high. Parachuting, on the other hand, was a method for swallowing the drug to speed up the absorption rate and avoid the crappy taste. You crush the pills into a powder, wrap the powder in single-ply toilet paper, and swallow the toilet paper. Twenty minutes later, my withdrawal symptoms were gone, or at least masked enough to get back to snorting lines of cocaine with a Sky Juice chaser.

I had the power to stop, I told myself.

But hey, no point in stopping on spring break.

That'd be just plain dumb.

8

BEFORE I GOT ON THE road for summer vacation, I swung by to pick up Sofia at her dorm—the breakup from months earlier didn't take. I was giving her a lift to the airport. I loaded a pile of her luggage into my trunk and we jumped on I-476, aiming for the Philadelphia International. I watched her board her flight, Philly to San Juan, nonstop and in no time, she'd be home.

One more stop. I drove north, back up near campus to visit a friend—a kid dabbling in Xanax and oxy. I picked up a handful of pills, and I was now primed for the two-hour drive home.

I wasn't back in New Vernon three days before I ran out of blues and needed a hookup. Didn't take long. I made some calls, old friends, friends of friends, and somehow I got around to Bridget. We'd met ages ago back at Harding Township School. She told me about her boyfriend, Derek, *he's a good guy*, all that, and Derek was suddenly my New Vernon connection.

Throughout May and June, I paced myself. A blue here, a blue there. Friends came over, I snorted a blue. Out to a movie, another blue. Sitting home, by myself, fuck it, a blue would sure make life more fun. Then I quit. Cold turkey. I just stopped. And this time was different. No physical withdrawal. In its place, however, was some funky mental stuff, like a weird cloud following me around. I couldn't shake it. My emotions ran high—love, rage, joy, grief—shit, I was all over the map. Then they'd flatline. Anger, anxiety, surprise, trust, it all vanished. Nothing.

In June, I started up again.

By early July, I was high every day. I drove down to campus a couple of times, met with friends, restocked, got high. And by late July, I was addicted, full-on, got-to-have-it addicted.

After an uneventful summer of blue snorting, I arrived back at school for my junior year. Problem was, I couldn't function without painkillers. Couldn't go a day without a blue or pink or pale green, and the cravings got worse with each week and month. I tried to stop. I did. I even dosed up on Suboxone, a med used specifically to take the punch out of opioid withdrawal.

Didn't work.

I needed lots of pills, and I needed them on a regular basis.

9/11 crept up on me quicker than usual this year. And I wanted to make the effort to respect my dad by not using on the day of his death.

Instead of focusing on the negative stuff regarding 9/11, I made it to my first class in the morning and spent some time afterwards getting food with friends. But my mind was preoccupied with getting high. I didn't want to get high. I really didn't.

I didn't even last two hours before driving over to my buddies' apartment and getting three blues after one of my afternoon classes. I crushed the three pills down on the back of my MacBook Pro, snorted them really quick, and then flipped over the computer and opened it to start watching 9/11 videos. I had become accustomed to not feeling or showing any emotion while watching these videos, but I made it a point to get extra numb before I started my daylong video viewing sessions.

I wasn't content buying from students on campus. The pills were pricey, dosages inconsistent, and given half a chance I'd get ripped off. Druggies—and here I include sellers—are not a particularly ethical bunch. I'd sold a few pills myself and was thinking seriously of upping my game.

First, I needed to cut out the middleman.

In walked Sahir. Well, it didn't happen like that. I met a guy who knew a guy who knew Reedy who knew Sahir. Reedy had taken me to Sahir's off campus apartment a couple of times. We got along. He liked me. Sahir knew a guy in Philly, said he'd introduce me.

I was in.

"What's his name?"

"Later."

"It's a secret?"

Sahir eyed me. "You can call him Meech."

Sahir was a Villanova grad student, so he said. Half the lowlifes in town claimed to be grad students. Some I believed, others not.

I was in class at Bartley Hall, the main building for the university's School of Business when Sahir texted me.

It's time to go.

I'm in Bartley. Pick me up?

Outside The Exchange. Two minutes.

The setup made sense, I guess. Older Villanova students like Sahir lived off campus and had cars. They had to get their pills from somewhere, and parts of Philadelphia, the way I heard it, were an open-air drug market. These pills didn't magically find their way onto campus. Someone sourced them. Another someone sold them face-to-face. And kids like me consumed them. Supply and demand 101.

Sahir pulled up in a BMW, the little one, with the windows tinted dark. I put my cigarette out and hopped in the front seat.

"Where we going?" I asked.

"West Philly."

Thirty minutes later, we slowed and pulled to the curb on Sansom Street.

We waited for the dealer. I imagined Bodie from *The Wire*.

Sahir was a cool guy, but he was also nervous, which made me nervous. He moved a hand slowly down to the buckle of the seatbelt. I looked down and saw he had a pistol or a handgun or whatever the proper term tucked low between the seat and the buckle. I didn't know guns at the time. It was black, short barrel, one of those checkered grips.

"We won't need that, right?" I asked.

"Today, middle of the day, probably not."

I took a breath.

"Better to be safe, though," he said.

I'm sure he was right, but it still didn't sit right with me.

"Where are we? What neighborhood?"

He looked around, "Spruce Hill." Then he stared at me. "We're good. Be glad this ain't Tioga-Nicetown or Fairhill. Or Strawberry Mansion. Shit."

Sure I liked oxy and codeine and Opana and a bunch of others. Who didn't? Up to now, it was all just good fun. Yet here I was with Sahir in far West Philly, one of us with a gun. All part of the college lifestyle, I told myself. Drive to the hood, do a little business, and get home in time to watch *Breaking Bad* on TV. In a way, Sahir, Philly, Sansom Street, it was an adrenaline rush. And I liked that people needed me, or needed oxy from me. I earned a few dollars in the process, and everyone was happy. I wasn't this big dealer. On the contrary, I was small time. Miniscule. But the buy, the transaction itself—it could sometimes be better than the high.

The guy showed up wearing skinny-ass black jeans, Timberland boots, and a North Face puffy jacket zipped up tight, a regular outdoorsman. Not what I expected. This was Meech, though he didn't say it.

Sahir did all the talking.

Meech leaned over so he could see inside the car, said, "Jawns." *Jawns, jaunts, Js,* all the same thing—Philly for oxycodone.

Sahir shrugged. "What else?"

"One hundred Js."

"At fifteen."

"Twenty," Meech said. "It's twenty, always twenty."

"Fine. One hundred at twenty." Sahir gripped two thousand dollars in his hand, five hundred of my own dough, mostly twenties, and put his hand and the money out the window.

Meech reached into his pocket and pulled out a baggie full of baby-blue pills, no way to know exactly how many inside. They did the deal. "See you around," Meech said, and walked away.

I took the baggie, counted out twenty-five pills, took two and put them back into the baggy and handed the baggy to Sahir.

The two pills, street price about sixty dollars, was payback for Sahir setting up the meet.

A month later, October, I was in Paris, there to visit my Villanova buddy, Grant, in the City of Lights studying political science. Sofia was with me. I'd snuck some Suboxone on the flight in a plastic bag. She'd be infuriated if she knew, but we were there for a week, and I couldn't go without. The trip was fun—Eiffel Tower, Champs-Élysées, The Louvre. We'd soaked up plenty of culture for one trip, combined with nonstop fighting over coffee and croissants every morning.

A day before we were scheduled to fly home, the hotel cleaning lady threw out my baggy of Suboxone. Not her fault, really. It looked like a nearly-empty plastic bag. No reason she would think otherwise.

Panic started to set in. Not long after, withdrawal set in.

I made a lame attempt to score something in a Paris pharmacy, but who was I kidding.

The flight back to Philadelphia was grueling, six hours of hell, in which I pretended to be flu-sick, or just-left-Paris sick, but definitely not painkiller withdrawal sick, in order to keep my relationship afloat.

By now, I had no desire to stay sober.

I'd lie, manipulate, deceive. I'd do anything to get and stay high.

For brief moments, I'd drift off, the body ache subsiding long enough to imagine my father, to wonder what he'd think of my life, of my uncanny ability to risk relationships, my university tenure, even jail time, perhaps, just to get high.

I thought of my father working at a pizza shop during college, or shoveling sidewalks in the winter to make an extra buck. And me, I had that same entrepreneurial spirit but honed it in on a successful, all-encompassing, drug-taking enterprise.

My roommate Fitzy was my best friend. I'd known him since fourth grade, 9/11. He made faces at me through the glass that separated our classroom from the corridor. So when Fitzy took me aside and told me my drug use had gotten out of control, I sort of had to listen.

"Listen, Boch, you're getting way out of control. You really need to stop doing blues, dude, just smoke weed like everyone else."

"I'm fine dude. Stop worrying about me."

"Dude, I'm worried about your life. What if your family finds out? Imagine if your dad were alive, dude."

The thing with Fitzy is I knew he cared. We went so far back that it wasn't like he had some sort of secondary motive for me to kick painkillers. Besides, what best friend would?

I loved Fitzy like a brother, and the thought of my dad made me want to cry. But I was too numb to cry. I thought about all the fun times me and Fitzy had as kids after my father died. His family lived on this big lake in town and we would always go out on this little boat, me, him and his dad, and catch bullfrogs. We would shine flashlights on his dad so the gnats and flies would be attracted to him and not us. I always wondered what it would be like to grow up with my dad, and what he would say along the way about stupid shit like girls and cars and sports. Would he think Sofia was worth it? Definitely not. Would he have guided me in the direction of a different sports car? Yeah, maybe a sweet Mercedes sedan or something like that. What would he think of the Yankees going under 500?

I tried quitting cold turkey. This was in our apartment in a small development called Home Properties of Bryn Mawr. Lots of red brick, windows lined up in a row, as good a place as any to turn things around. This was sometime before Christmas, and if the place was good, the timing was bad. People kill themselves around the holidays. Throw in a little self-applied drug rehab and no telling what I'd do.

I suffered through withdrawal for a few days, ready to strangle anyone within arm's reach, and then I spoke with a buddy at Saint Joseph's University. This guy knew his shit and told me to taper down my oxy intake before going cold. So I tried that. I was taking six pills a day. I'd cut it back to five, *okay*, four, and see how it went.

The thing was, I took three and wanted four. I took four and wanted five. Something wasn't adding up.

On the school's official Christmas break, I tried quitting again. This time at home. Didn't even come close. In fact, things got worse in that my tolerance kept stretching. I needed more and more to get the same old buzz.

For a long time, I gave up quitting.

When spring break rolled around, I hopped an airplane to the Dominican Republic. Lots of Villanova University kids and everyone in Fiji who could make it. We stayed at another crappy hotel in Punta Cana, right on the tippy-tip east end of the island. The view from our room overlooking both the Caribbean Sea *and* the Atlantic Ocean, or so the brochure said.

This time, I smuggled in ninety blues. I figured a week on the Coconut Coast, I'd inhale seventy pills. That left twenty if I miscalculated. Some other sneaks pirated in Klonopin, an anxiety med, and I sucked up all my body could handle. And the Dominican Republic was rife with cocaine, pure, chalky, and expensive.

Cocaine and Klonopin were better than oxy, right? Each line of cocaine was one less line of my precious, limited supply of oxy. But even with the substitutes, I still ran out of oxycodone before my last day there, which naturally put me in a panic.

I texted a friend, Tim, asked him to pick me up at Newark Liberty International Airport and make sure he had pills in hand. When I landed, I turned my phone on to a bombardment of text messages and calls. Most said some version of this: *Did I hear about Billy?*

Short answer: No.

Billy Zimmermann was a friend from Seton Hall Prep and a Villanova classmate.

I was in a bad way. I'd deal with whatever it was later.

I got into Tim's car. Said, "You got the Js I asked about?"

"Hello to you, too."

"I know," I said, shaking my head.

He handed me two pills. I wrapped the pills together in a dollar bill, like a present, crushed the pills with a lighter and opened the dollar bill to a bluish powder, as excited as a Christmas morning, and snorted the powder in a fluid practiced motion.

On the ride home, I called an old friend. She had just texted me, asking if I'd heard about Billy. "Matty," she said, her voice staggering. "I don't know how to say this. Billy is dead."

"Holy shit. I'm stunned," I said. I'm not ready for this, I thought to myself.

"I'm so sorry."

I couldn't believe it, and I sure as hell didn't know what to say. Apparently, Billy was down in Mexico in a rental with three others, when whoever was driving missed the exit, made a U-turn on the highway, and a large truck t-boned them. Billy died on the spot. The others were hurt bad.

Billy was gone, and here I was getting high.

A slow high—not my usual.

I turned to Tim and said, "Answer me this. Why do bad things happen to good people?"

Tim gave me an odd look, assessing me. "Let me get you home."

I was close to tears. Billy and I both played soccer at the Prep. When he came to Villanova, I tried getting him to join Fiji. Instead, he joined Phi Sig, a fraternity we were close with. He was such a genuine, happy person that I was lucky to call him a friend. His smile would light up a room in a heartbeat.

Billy Z. was gone.

I had some blues hidden at home. That'd take the edge off.

9

I SHOWED UP HIGH TO Billy's wake.

After the wake, and before the funeral, I took a little blue, not a big one.

I walked into the funeral home with my buddy Dan at my side. Both of our dads worked at Cantor Fitzgerald. Both long dead. I approached Billy's parents, said something I don't remember, blubbering, high as the fucking Goodyear blimp, and made a fool of myself, slurring my words. I said my condolences, an expression of sympathy, no idea what was coming out of my mouth.

Dan grabbed my arm, pulled me aside. "Bocchi." He gave me a look.

"Dan," I said. Even this one word came out wrong, like I had too many Sour Patch Kids in my mouth, all that sour messing with my tongue and lips.

"Can you hear yourself? 'Cause I can, and you're mumbling. Your words are garbled. Bad."

Not just my words, my head. My brain was a mushy mess.

"You got to get your shit together," he insisted.

I looked off, thinking about nothing. I cried, but it also seemed like forced tears. I felt the feelings and emotions, of course, but I had to push them out. I mean, I was genuinely crushed by Billy's death, but I felt empty inside. The numbness completely overrode a true connection between my brain and behaviors. There was a void I could never seem to fill.

I couldn't let myself be vulnerable. Not enough to express my true emotions, if I could even remember what they were. I was desperate. Desperate to know the story of my father's death, desperate to forget what my uncle did to me. At home, before the wake, I cried like a baby. Then I inhaled an oxycodone. That was better. No pain. Or, it was there, I suppose, but it had a far-off quality to it.

Call it delusional, call it crazy, call it whatever you want to call it. Even though I had concrete evidence of how my dad died, I still wanted to know more. I only knew the few things for sure: phone call with mom, phone call with Peter, phone call with Uncle Tony, and the end results. There had to be more to my father's story. I *needed* to find his story. So I might have been high all the time, but I could still hone in and focus on my research.

I had texted Uncle Tony, asking him to regurgitate the same story to me once again. "Did you hear anything in the background, people screaming anything like that?"

"No, dude, nothing at all."

"And his voice, it was calm? He didn't sound scared?"

"No, not at all."

About this time, I added Xanax—xannies—to the mix, a medication used to treat anxiety disorders, a sedative, and here's the kicker, the drug itself could cause paranoid or suicidal ideation, toy with your memory, judgment, and coordination. Pop a Xanax and down a couple of beers; the combination slowed my breathing, put me in a drug-induced Zen state.

I told myself no one noticed.

Not true.

My brothers noticed. Even fourteen-year-old Michael.

I used to play *FIFA* with Michael. I'd be high much of the time. Then I got to where I'd play *only* if I was high, blues, xannies, whatever.

I was busy. I was selling at the time, still not a lot, but people wanted what they wanted and they wanted it now. That meant I was forever buying or setting up a buy. When working on a buy, the last thing I cared about was hanging out with my brothers.

A few days after Billy's funeral, I needed to make a buy, so I made some calls, walking up to my room, my voice hushed.

Michael saw me, his big eyes getting bigger, he said, "You want to play *FIFA*?"

I showed him the cell phone in my hand. Mouthed the words, "I'm on the phone."

"We can do best out of seven."

I took another step. I pulled the phone from my ear, "Michael, I'm on the phone."

"I'll get it set up."

"Fine," I said. "I'll be down in five minutes."

"Can we start now?"

"Five minutes."

An hour later, I returned downstairs. Time disappeared when I set up a deal. I was waiting on a call from a seller. I was low on pills. I needed to move the moment he called. Otherwise, the whole deal would take another day or two.

Michael and I were picking our teams when I got the callback. "I have to go. This stinks, I know. I'm sorry. I'll play later. Promise."

"When?"

"When I'm back."

"When?"

"Before you have to go to bed," I said.

"I don't know."

"Way before. I promise. Really."

"I love you," he said.

"I love you too, Mikey."

I said all the right words. I'd had lots of practice. I knew what to say to my little brother to make him happy. Didn't matter I'd never follow through. We were family. I was a junior at Villanova goddamn University. I'd been places, traveled, knew how to talk to people. I was smart and charming and handsome. And all that, in my mind, gave me the leeway to say and do whatever I wanted.

So I did the deal and got high and walked in the door four hours later.

Michael was in bed.

In the morning, he was notably unsympathetic to my bullshit.

As for Nick and Paul, Nick knew about the drugs but never said a word.

Paul, the youngest, had no idea. Ten at the time, I even took him on a buy with me. I was home for the weekend, no one in the house but Paul and me. A big brother surveilling a little brother. Paul was innocent, kind of immature, I don't know. The kind of kid who needed an eye on him.

I waited on a call from Derek. I'd get the okay that he had a handful of blues and then skedaddle out the door. That was if my mother got home in time to take Paul off my hands. I knew deep down she'd never make it in time. I could maybe zip out and do the deal and get back before she got home. Maybe. Or I could zip out and she'd show up the next minute and I'd be in deep shit.

I stared at my phone, hoping I'd missed a call. Nothing. I put the phone in my pocket, shouted to the TV room, "Hey, are you up for a drive?"

"Huh?" Paul was watching cartoons. Eyes forward, his thin neck leaning into the TV, all his attention on this tall blue jay and a short raccoon, one or both forever mowing the lawn. The blue jay pushed a mower, and the raccoon sat on the engine with a pot of coffee in his hand. Not my thing.

"Turn it off," I said. "We're going for a ride."

Paul finally looked away, now sort of excited. "Where we going?"

"I left my phone charger at my buddy's. After, we can see a movie, I guess."

"Can I bring my iPad?"

"To the movie?"

He was already reaching for the iPad.

"Sure, buddy," I said. "Let's go."

We drove up 287 to Derek's place, Paul head down playing a game on his iPad the whole ride. The kid never once looked out the window. Just as well—as I didn't want him recalling this little excursion if he was grilled later.

Briefly, I thought back to the times when I would drive around with my dad in his Porsche. I would sit in the right back seat, amazed by how he would switch gears so fast, and then peer out the window as we sped by cars on the road. Sometimes I would forget where we were going, but I felt safe with my dad.

We neared Derek's. I parked on the side street because my drug connection would be rightfully pissed if he saw that I'd invited family.

I said, "I'll be right back. Don't go anywhere. I mean it." Paul didn't even look up. "Really," I said. "Don't get out of the car. Are you listening?"

He lifted his little head and looked around. "Why can't I get out?"

"Just don't," I said.

I felt bad about leaving my little brother in the car. This wasn't the hood, but still. Something gurgled in my stomach, some body sign that I was up to no good. Fuck it. I needed my pills.

I ran down one street and over and up the drive, knocked, then pushed open the door. Derek was there, a baggie of pills in his hand. I grabbed the baggie, counted twelve blues, pinched out two, crushed and snorted them. I was an expert. Didn't take sixty seconds. Thirty seconds later I felt way better, most of the urgency evaporating, my nerves settled. When Derek invited me to smoke a blunt, I knew I should say no, knew on some far-off level I was shirking my responsibilities as baby-brother-watcher. When he lit the thing, I took it between my fingers and inhaled and without realizing we shuffled down the hall into the TV room. When he lit the second blunt, I'd all but forgotten I had a little brother, much less one in the car around the corner. By the time he lit the third, I don't know, I was just high.

Sometime later, I got up off the couch, stood in place until I stopped wobbling, and walked outside to my car.

Paul was still there minding his business, thumbs and fingers tapping away at his iPad, as if I'd never left. I sat and buckled up and started the car. He asked, "What movie we seeing?" His squeaky, innocent voice gave off a lackadaisical feel. He was completely unaware that I was gone for nearly thirty minutes.

"Another time, buddy."

"Oh," he said.

"I got an idea. How about we stop and buy some candy, stay up late. Maybe watch *Family Guy*?"

"Okay."

If my brothers were oblivious or even accepting of my erratic conduct, my mother was a different animal.

She witnessed my transformation from a caring, punctual son to the oxy- and coke-snorting, Xanax-popping junkbox I'd turned into. The odd behavior and sneakiness and general disrespect for family activities didn't raise any red flags. My spending habits did. I blew through cash like it was confetti. She had access to my checking account, occasionally looked at a statement, didn't like what she saw, and confronted me. It's what good parents do, right?

"Are you doing drugs?" she asked me.

"Mom."

"I'd like a straight answer."

"This is stupid. It's the money, right? I'm spending too much. I agree. I'll do better. The kids at Nova...you don't understand. You think I spend money, you should see."

"Matthew."

"No. I'm not doing drugs. I wouldn't do that."

She would be mortified if she found her eldest son was addicted to drugs. Even so, I wanted to say yes. But I didn't have the balls. I was embarrassed. I was afraid.

I thought about what my dad would have done, would have said if he were alive. He would've been furious, but he also would reassure me everything would be okay. Maybe he would beat my ass but, honestly, I didn't know. I didn't want to admit I had a problem. A big problem. A huge, monstrous, shit-for-brains, stupid problem. I couldn't do that.

She cut my allowance, a little pruning of the money she normally dumped into my account, and now I had a very serious, tangible complication. I needed money to buy, so I could sell and make a little money to buy and sell and buy again, and...well, you get the idea.

So, I stole her debit card. I guessed at her pin, which was not so hard to figure out.

I'd get caught. Eventually. I knew that. But I still didn't care.

The first time I did it, she didn't say anything. Moms are so forgiving.

The next time, she said, "I want to ask you something. Be honest with me. Can you do that?"

"Of course." I had a look of genuine concern on my face.

"Did you take my debit card?" She had the offending card in her hand.

"No. I did not."

"Look at these charges." She pushed the statement at me. She'd underlined three charges.

Three ATM withdrawals—$200, $200, and $80—all of it spent on oxycodone. I knew her ATM habits. She typically withdrew money in $200 increments. So, I withdrew $200 a couple of times and she didn't notice. The $80 withdrawal fucked me up.

Stupid, really. A cry for help, perhaps? A laughable, half-baked cry for help, if you asked me. That said, if it did the job, I might consider it an intelligent, astute, even imaginative (given that at first glance, it appeared so lame) attention-grabber.

She rattled the bank statement at me again.

"Mom," I said, "this is crazy."

"Did you?"

"I have no idea what those are," I said.

"Did you? Tell me."

"I don't know what to say."

"Be honest. Is that so hard? Are you doing drugs?"

I took a breath. "Okay," I said. "Okay, here it is. You want to hear.... Let me start over. I'm addicted to painkillers," I said.

It felt so good to finally say it out loud.

"Tell me again," she said.

"I'm addicted to painkillers."

"This is the truth?"

"Yes."

"Oh, Matthew. I love you so much, honey. We're going to get you help."

10

BEFORE MY MOTHER COULD ARRANGE to get me committed to a drug detox where they would, I was sure, flush the bad habits out of me, I hit up Derek one last time.

We said our hellos and within three minutes had snorted several blues and popped a few bars (a cute moniker for Xanax, 2 milligram pills, that sort of resembled bars). We stood and shuffled to the leather couch. We sat hard and leaned back and extended our legs. Life was good. A favorite ritual of ours—get high and chill on the couch watching mindless TV and smoking blunts.

My phone vibrated.

The caller ID said it was my grandfather, Nonno.

I wanted to answer it. I did.

I hadn't talked to him in a while. I should answer. I should.

But I was high, so I didn't. I put my phone back in my pocket. A moment later, it vibrated again. He'd left a voicemail. "Hello. It's me." Pause. His voice weathered, rumbly, the way old people's voices got. "Matthew, it's me, Nonno. I wanted to say I'm thinking about you." Some breathing, another pause. "I love you. Okay, Coco Bello. I'll talk to you soon. *Ti amo*, Matteo. *Ciao, ciao.*"

Nonno always left me the nicest voicemails.

A day later, I drove seven miles south to Sunrise Detox—*a new beginning*, the slogan said. The place was all of thirteen minutes away if I drove slowly. Was it a good facility? Who knew? It was close.

I parked. Locked my Jeep, a classy black Grand Cherokee. Checked myself in.

The thing was, I had no desire to stop taking drugs.

In fact, I checked in thinking I could get a nice oil change, update my fluids, refresh my spiritual self-talk, that kind of thing, and come out with a much lower tolerance, and—drumroll please—I could inhale the same four or five pills a day but get way higher.

The treatment lasted seven days.

Days one through five were pretty much what you'd expect. Shitting my brains out, vomiting stomach bile, horrible anxiety. All of it.

Day six, my counselor Vicky, a nice woman with glasses, called me into her office and said I had a phone call. This wasn't good. We were only allowed calls to family within clearly defined hours. This wasn't one of those hours.

My mother said, "Nonno passed away."

Her voice was more callous than I expected, maybe preparing herself for the days ahead. "A heart attack," she said. "No one knows for sure. I wanted you to know. You two were close." I heard some sniffing. "I wanted you to know is all. I'll call later. I love you."

The call had ended before I even said goodbye.

Nonno was gone.

Fuck.

I had no serious plans to stay sober after detox. After only a week dry, does anyone? At a minimum, I'd drink and smoke weed.

On day six, I stopped taking the Suboxone the doctors prescribed. Suboxone slowed me down. I was a planner, and I planned to do blues the moment I was released, and the Suboxone in my system would only mess with my high.

Day seven, I got out.

I climbed in my SUV, so happy I cried all the way home. Really. I was elated to be free. I felt I'd been in jail, locked up without a say in the matter. That I'd volunteered for the lockup didn't figure into things.

I got home and hugged my mom, bawling at the sight of me—the way moms do.

I said I was having lunch with my friends. "Do you have any cash?"

She handed me whatever was in her wallet.

Then I drove to Hoboken, met up with Helen, my new best friend from Sunrise Detox, and bought four blues at twenty dollars a pop.

I felt bad lying to my mother.

I did it anyway. It's what addicts do.

After detox, I did what I do best. I snorted pills like no tomorrow.

And the whole time, my mother thought I was sober. I played along because I didn't want to worry her.

I attended Nonno's wake. High, of course. I had a good number of pills in my pocket to get me through the service. I loved my grandfather more than anything. We bonded over so many things. We talked soccer—Juventus F.C., a professional Italian football club we followed based in Turin. We talked girls and wine, and he shared plenty of stories about his World War II experiences. Captured by the Germans at sixteen, he was forced to work in a labor camp used to house enemies of the state, meaning Italians and people of other nationalities Hitler didn't like. Nonno endured brutal conditions, beatings, bad weather, and meaningless work day after day. His prisoner of war number was 911.

Nonno also told stories of my father, how he worked three jobs to get himself through college, how he made his way from the mailroom at a law firm to a managing director at Cantor. When he spoke of my father, I saw the love in his eyes. And I believe he must have seen the same in mine. My father was the oldest son. I was the oldest grandson. It all felt right.

Nonno always saw the good in me, and he always stressed how important it was to love my family, take care of my mother, and carry the Bocchi name proudly. Besides my uncle Tony, the Bocchi name was on my brothers and I, particularly me, at this moment. Both Nonno and my dad would be mortified, knowing that I was carrying the Bocchi name while high as a kite.

I spent much of the wake doing two things: calling my new best friend, Helen, and checking my phone for a callback from Helen.

She was a nurse, late twenties, cute with a fake tan and fake nails. She drove a Mercedes-Benz. Had her own prescription for oxycodone, and thus a perpetual yet not limitless supply. In addition to the oxy, she had access to other prescription meds. A nurse with sticky fingers.

On one of my calls, I actually got through. "Helen, are you going to be ready? I'm out of here in forty minutes."

"A funeral—that's where you're at?"

"The wake. Doesn't matter. Are we set?"

"I'm waiting on people, but yes, or probably."

I waited ten minutes and then called again. "It's me."

"You know, you're starting to annoy me," she said and hung up.

Ten minutes later, I did it again. "Anything? Wait, don't hang up. I'm sorry, I'm just on edge, the funeral—I mean wake—and all. Wait, wait. I almost hate to ask. I need some xannies. Please."

"I'll make it happen," she said. "Text me when you're heading back home."

"Yeah, yeah. No, wait. You text me when you have the pills."

She was exasperated, said, "What did I expect," referring, I think, to the over-eager, anxious lugheads you hook up with in detox.

I sat down next to my grandmother, Nonna, a drag because she couldn't stop crying. I held her, and cried right along with her, and checked for text messages every twenty seconds.

Fifteen minutes later, *victory*. Helen had the pills in her hands.

That out of the way, I sort of fell apart. Time to let the emotions fly, which was only possible because I hadn't taken enough blues to get numb. After detox, I wanted to maintain a balance of being high and coherent enough to feel the world around me. So far, so good.

Then someone I didn't know stood behind a podium and said something I didn't hear. Next, it was my father's siblings' turns—Diane, Lucy, Anna, and Tony. My cousins followed. As the oldest grandson, most people expected me to say something too. I thought I would, though I planned to keep my comments short. Then I changed my mind. I had the pills waiting, and any delay was way too long.

I imagined myself standing behind the podium, then going off on some riff about Nonno being the greatest, adding some touching story of whatever for color, and getting sentimental and teary. A fleeting memory came to me of my dad speaking in front of the town on Memorial Day in 2001. He spoke about how it was important to honor those who served and died for our country, and what it meant to be a hero.

In the current moment though, I realized I'd have a room full of relatives corralling me, wanting to share their own unending stories, or they'd dawdle over me, in a time-consuming attempt to make things all better.

Rather than get sucked into the momentum of these things, I just up and left. I went home, changed clothes, hopped in my Jeep, and hit the road to Hoboken.

About this time, I watched a documentary, *Voices from Inside the Towers*. By now, I was numb to the photos and videos of the attacks. What I hadn't considered was the audio record, what amounted to thousands, maybe tens of thousands, of calls, some pleading for help, a few documenting what they saw with remarkable clarity, and others using few words to say goodbye.

Many of the recorded calls confirmed that conditions inside the towers were so difficult people had few choices: choke, burn, get trampled on the way down. Or jump. Some two minutes after the massive American Airlines Boeing 767 hit the north tower, people began jumping from the floors above the crash site. First one, then another, then dozens, perhaps hundreds, leaped or fell to their deaths from the burning tower. They landed on the hard pavement, the tops of parked cars, rooftops of adjacent buildings.

According to the narrator, temperatures inside the towers spiked as burning jet fuel and smoke turned the upper floors into a chimney. Given the increasingly difficult conditions, people began breaking windows. At first, they wanted fresh air.

I heard it in their voices.

When the heat increased, they wanted out.

I still had two months left of spring semester when my mother hinted that maybe I should take a break. Drop out. Stay home. She used the words "medical leave." I told her it was important for me to finish the semester. I told her I'd started something and it was in my nature to finish what I'd started. What mother could stand up to such an argument, such a declaration of character and can-do spirit?

"If that's how you feel," she said. "I'll support you."

Candidly, I just wanted to be with my girlfriend, Sofia. And she wanted to be with me, so she said. I learned later she'd been dating around, a couple of guys, all's fair in lust as we were "taking a break" during my detox. Now that I was back, cleansed in her mind, and my weaknesses given a good scrub, we picked up where we left off.

In truth, the real truth, I wanted to return to school for the lifestyle, the atmosphere. I wanted fraternity parties and loud music and so many bodies crammed in a room you couldn't breathe. And drugs. I really wanted drugs.

In a matter of days, I was out of control.

I bought drugs and consumed them. Bought more. Consumed more. I couldn't get enough. And while it was relatively easy to hide my drug habit, it was impossible to hide my spending habit.

In April, I overdrew one of my accounts. My mother had a handful of accounts at Barrington Aldrich, and when I started at Villanova, she opened another one, a checking account for me to cover food and books and general necessities. She handed me a debit card and told me to use it wisely. The upside was because my account was connected to hers, I instantly had a whopping overdraft limit of several thousand dollars. How many thousands, I wasn't entirely sure.

Once I'd overdrawn the account, an assistant at the firm, Susan, would shoot me an email. If I didn't respond quickly with some plausible scheme to transfer monies around and right the scales, Susan would call my mother.

On a beautiful April afternoon, I was on my way to meet Meech, my connection in Philly, on the corner of North 19th Street and Poplar Street, across from the post office. Three blocks from Eastern State Penitentiary. Meech was holding a batch of blues for me. A done deal. That's when my mom texted me and said I'd apparently overdrawn my account by two thousand dollars.

That can't be right, I texted.

Susan is never wrong.

I'm in the middle of something. Can I call you later?

She immediately called me, a tone of seriousness I had never heard before.

"Are you doing the pills again?"

"It's not fair to accuse me of pills every time we have an issue about money."

"Are you?"

"Mom."

"Are you?"

"I won't lie to you, yes. I mean, no, not really."

"Are you high this minute? You're not making sense."

"I *had* been taking a pill every once in a while, but I stopped and I'm doing better now."

"If he knew," she said, "your father would be devastated."

She was right, of course. But if he were around, would I be on my way to Philly?

My junior year ended, and I was sort of sad to see it go. In May, I hightailed it out of Bryn Mawr, and I enjoyed a breezy two-hour drive north. When I arrived in New Vernon, no one was home, already away on a previously planned vacation. A couple of days by myself would do me some good.

That evening, I went to the Schwartzes' for a party. The Schwartz kids were twins, my age, Kyle and Jake, with a younger sister Hillary. I'd known them forever. They'd invited Fitzy, Nicky, and some others I forget. We did what kids my age always did our first night back in town. We drank and smoked pot. I inhaled blues and some xannies and proceeded to get blackout high.

Then I made a joke about Hillary, called her a princess, but apparently had this kind of shitty look on my face when I said it. The blues and the shitty look combined, and suddenly everyone, including Hillary, thought I was trashing our host. I wasn't. Or, at least, I don't think I was. Impossible to know when you're so high you can't remember what you said sixty seconds ago.

That's when her brothers ganged up on me, shouting at me to stop shouting at them. I stormed outside where Kyle caught up with me and tried to talk some sense into me, begging me to stay over. I was in no condition to drive, and I knew it, but I still jumped in my Jeep and started the engine. That's when Kyle hustled around to the front of the SUV and stood his ground.

I revved the engine.

He put both hands on the hood, a sort of comic gesture, but I got the point.

I shouted through the windshield, "Move out of the fucking way."

"Come back inside, Boch. Seriously, man."

I paused a beat. "Fine," I shouted.

Kyle moved to the side of the SUV, and I promptly cranked the wheel, hit the gas, and spun the car onto the lawn. In the process, I nearly ran over Kyle, who was quicker on his feet than I knew. One of my best friends since fourth grade, and in a moment of anger or madness or whatever, I'd nearly flattened him in his own front yard.

I made it home without incident, a minor miracle given my state, stumbled into the TV room, and passed out on the couch.

In the morning, I rolled over, and Fitzy was rubbing my arm. "Wake up. Boch, you okay? Wake up."

I was still high, lying on my side, angry. At what I had no idea. I saw Fitzy and Kyle and Jake and Nicky. "What the fuck are you guys doing here?"

Fitzy said, "We were worried."

Nicky, a kid who never said anything, stood there and shook his head like he was supremely disappointed in me. Kyle and Jake were off to the side, staring at me, no longer mad at me, each with a bland expression—sort of old-man-ish and nurturing.

It hit me then. "Oh, fuck. Is this some kind of fucking intervention?"

Kyle looked nervous, uncomfortable with whatever this was. "If you want us to leave—"

Fitzy said, "We're not going anywhere."

"You said you were worried," I said. "Well, here I fucking am."

Kyle spoke softly, some goddamn tricky intervention technique, said, "Can you please stop saying 'fuck'?"

It was a strange request—Kyle's known me my whole life, and I've always cursed a lot. Maybe he thought I was making light of the situation, which I obviously was.

"Fuck," I said and we all sort of laughed. I sat upright on the couch, a bit dizzy. I looked up at Fitzy. I liked him, trusted him. He was a tall kid, fucking huge smile, and when he let loose with those big teeth of his, he was hard to resist.

"You were pretty messed up," Fitzy said. "Then you got in your Jeep and sped off. We were worried."

I felt for my baggie of blues in my pocket, nothing in it. "My Jeep...I can do what I want."

"This is me, dude," Fitzy said. "You need to get some help."

I was about to say *fuck off* but held onto it. Man, I was dizzy.

Fitzy said, "We all love you. Keep this up—you're going to kill yourself."

Kyle had tears in his eyes. Not the big kind, the other, the red-eye watery kind, a puddle on his lower lid just about to break loose.

"Right, right," I said. I looked around at my friends. "Is this really happening? Give me a second to think. Okay, okay. I need help. Okay. I'll get some help."

I had no desire to get help. I knew it, and deep down, they probably knew it too. But it didn't hurt to just say what they wanted to hear. Withdrawals were looming in the shadows.

"We're here for you," Fitzy said.

"The thing is, I need my pills. I really need them. I'm out and I need more. It's a dependency thing. I need them."

Nicky said nothing.

Kyle said, "What are you saying?"

"Before I go anywhere, a detox, rehab, whatever, I need pills."

Kyle said, "Fine. We'll go with you. Where to?"

"Hoboken," I said. "You don't have to come. I'll go, then tomorrow I'll, I don't know. We'll figure it out tomorrow."

Jake thought about it, a considerate person, said, "We'll come. Then you stay at our house for the night."

So off we went on an early morning drug run to Hoboken.

When we got to Helen's, I hopped out of the car. I had a straw in my pocket. The straw was important. With a straw, I could speed up the process. I could take a few pills, drop them inside the straw, fold one end so the pills didn't fall out, and chew on the straw until the pills were dust. Once I had a powder, I'd put the straw in my nose and take a big nasally inhale.

I met Helen in a parking garage, did the exchange, and the thing with the straw. I got back to the car and gently lifted one of the little blue pills out of the baggie.

"Just one," Fitzy said.

"Yes." I said, "Just one."

I snorted it. I was supposed to be in withdrawal or so they thought, so I pretended as if that one blue was a lifesaver.

"Thanks," I said. "I appreciate you guys more than you know."

Jake reached out his hand. "Here," he said.

I handed him the baggie with all my pills. I'd briefly considered fighting it, make up some shit about holding onto the bag, a security blanket, how I needed them to trust me to hold my own shit, but thought better of it.

That night, Jake mercifully handed over one more little blue pill.

Then my favorite twin in the whole world flushed the rest of my pills down the toilet.

I snorted almost 300 milligrams of oxycodone a day. A couple of pills would wear off way too soon. In the morning, I pleaded for more. Withdrawal kicked in and I was unbearable, constantly walking around their yard with restlessness and anxiety. But Jake and Kyle didn't give in.

My mother returned from the beach and drove straight to the Schwartzes' house. I was outside in the driveway chain-smoking when she arrived. She went inside and chatted with Mrs. Schwartz, now going by her maiden name, Ms. Williams, since the divorce.

We drove home, not a pill in the place. I walked outside onto the patio, sat on a wooden chair, dope-sick, miserable, gloomy, and I smoked one cigarette after another. My mother came outside and moved close and stood still, staring at me. That's when I told her I wanted detox. If I had the energy to shed a tear, I would have. My voice was pleading. I begged and implored. I really wanted it, I told her. I'd seen the error of my ways, and I needed help.

It just occurred to me that maybe it happened the other way around. Maybe she got home from a dreamy vacation, found her oldest son stinking of cigarettes, pale, gaunt, and way too skinny, all obvious signs I'd just returned from a bender and being a conscientious mother used to carrying the load, she all but ordered me into detox.

It could have happened that way.

I said, "Don't tell my brothers."

"Why is this?"

"Okay, let me tell Nick. The others are too young. They wouldn't understand."

"Your second detox...you think this is so difficult to understand?"

"Mom."

"Fine."

Later that day I talked to Nick, just a couple of years younger than me. Well, I tried to talk to him, but I chickened out. So I texted him. *I've got something to tell you.*

What?

I stared at the floor, ashamed, even as I typed. *I've been doing oxy again. I'm going to detox, as soon as Mom can find a place. I just wanted you to know. I'm not telling Michael and Paul. Not now.*

You're pathetic, dude.

What?

Get the help you need. Seriously.

I didn't respond. Instead, I forwarded the text to my mom. I did it to make her feel bad. I'm the victim here, right?

I don't think it worked.

She made some calls but couldn't get me into an inpatient detox—a lockup, which was what I needed. They were all booked up with other early-summer oxy-burnouts and crank heads and pill connoisseurs. She'd try again tomorrow.

When I was a kid, I was obsessed with Batman. My dad had gotten me tons of Batman toys, and Nick and I would always dress up as Batman and Robin. I watched all of the movies and the cartoons over and over...I couldn't get enough Batman. On my birthday one year, my dad came home dressed up as Batman. I had no idea it was my dad. I just assumed he was still at work.

He picked me up and swung me around, throwing me in the air and catching me as I fell back down.

Here I was thinking about it again, hoping this superhero father would come and rescue me again.

Without my pills, I slipped quickly into withdrawal—I mean, quickly into *hell*. I had all the normal symptoms: aches, chills, sweats, nausea, yawning. And a new one: I couldn't stop my legs from shaking.

I woke, puked in my bathroom sink, walked downstairs where my mother was making breakfast. I yawned, mouth open as wide as it would go. I took a breath and yelled, "Where are the fucking pills?"

She didn't know how to react. "Matthew."

I was desperate. The goddamn Schwartz brothers had flushed my stash, yet I had it in my head Ms. Williams had given some of the pills to my mom. One mother to another sort of thing. Didn't have to make sense, I just wanted my fucking little blue pills.

"Honey..." she said.

"I need those pills." I was teary-eyed, face burning, blood pressure off the goddamn charts. I grabbed her hand and put it over my heart. "Feel this," I shouted as if it was her fault. I pressed harder until I felt the thump through her hand, a faltering irregular beat not meant for hearts.

"Whatever pills you think I have, I don't."

I yawned. "Ms. Williams, she didn't...you don't have one pill?"

"What does Daisy have to do with this?"

I yawned again. I shouted, "I can't breathe."

She had a spatula in her hand, some egg on it, and I saw the uncooked egg and gagged. She put the spatula on the counter. "Slow down. Breathe. You'll be all right."

"I know you have them."

She patted me on the back. "We'll get past this."

I shouted, "Stop being a bitch. I need them."

Now she was just sad. "Go on upstairs. Pack a bag. Let me make some calls."

She finally got me into a detox. The place was run by a somewhat attractive nut who believed in the power of outpatient detox. Spend the day with us and get clean. I arrived at eight in the morning and left at eight at night for seven straight days.

It would never work; I knew it from the start.

Okay, so the chief medical director had put in her time, a residency in Psychiatry at Johns Hopkins in Baltimore, on and on, but she was still a nut to trust users like me to be responsible members of society once we left the building.

I was prescribed Suboxone to help reduce the withdrawal, but after a couple of days, I walked away from the med counter and spat out the little orange sublingual strip and pocketed it. Why? Because if I took Suboxone in the morning, I couldn't get high at night, or at least not the quality high I'd come to expect.

11

I MASTERED THE ART OF only getting high at night.

Like a martini after work.

In June, I started an internship with Concord Trust, corner of Lexington Avenue and East 44th Street in New York City, where I worked on a trading desk. The hours were glacial, and soon, I couldn't get through the workday without a little pick me up. I would get in the office at seven and wouldn't leave until seven, and that didn't include the commute home, let alone time to score more drugs after work. Then I found a drug delivery service. These guys actually dispatched some of the best coke in the city to the building's front door for three hundred dollars an eight ball. That's when I abandoned my nights-only resolution and started getting high at work.

Concord Trust was a British firm—investment banking, equities, alternative finance, that kind of thing. I was able to land the internship through a family friend who put in a good word for me. The role was similar to what my father did back in the day before becoming a broker. He would be proud that I had the desire to start off somewhere in finance, but given the fact that he worked his ass off in the mailroom just to get a shot at being on a desk at some point, he'd be pissed I was able to land a position so easily without any hard work or effort.

My manager asked if I'd mind working British trading hours, two-thirty a.m. to twelve noon.

Sure, why not?

For no discernable reason, I chose to make the changeover from days to nights mid-week. On Wednesday, I went to work at eight in the morning, put in a long day, and then grabbed dinner and a handful of beers with some friends in Midtown. Next, I picked up a baggie of cocaine, a cute little see-through plastic thingy with a thin red line across the top, did a couple of lines, and on to Emily's dorm room for a little sleep.

I knew Emily from Villanova. We were just a hookup, nothing long-term. A Monday-to-Friday thing. She finagled a summer rental in one of the residence halls at NYU, blocks from Washington Square Park, a place I'd never been.

I hailed a taxi for a sluggish thirty-minute ride to Rubin Hall.

I sat on the bed, breathed slowly, willing my body to quiet itself. I lay down—fully clothed, mind you, but it didn't matter. I'd only nap for an hour or so, but I couldn't sleep. Too much cocaine. Better, I thought, to charge off to Concord Trust and catch up on a little homework for an online course I was taking. I'd start my new hours at two-thirty a.m. but got back to the office around midnight.

The New York location was small. The trading floor had two lonely trading tables, long wooden things, dozens of screens stacked three high, ten people to a table. There were a bunch of offices around the perimeter. Occasionally, a Brit traveling through NYC used one of the offices for a few days.

I finished my homework at one a.m., took an online quiz, scored an A, and celebrated by slipping off to one of the elegant bathroom stalls to snort a line of cocaine. I held the baggie in my hand, squeezed the corners to sprinkle some cocaine on top of the toilet paper holder. The smell of gasoline emerged as I poured it out—it was extremely chalky, sticking to my credit card as I formed the obtuse line.

I quickly inhaled the line. My nose burned as the cocaine entered my nasal cavity and rinsed down my throat.

Back at my desk, I was tired, bone-weary. I counted the hours. I'd been up for twenty hours straight. Throw in too many beers, a few lines of cocaine, and at least three blue pills through-out the day, and my body had all but given out. I put my head down, just for a moment, and fell asleep. I woke when I heard one of the night traders tromping into the office. Elliott, a nice guy, sat at the desk next to me.

A typical trading desk had from three to nine large screens set up in a kind of shallow curve. Each screen displayed some critical bit of trading data—news, market movers, stock volume, oversold indicators, specialized trading software, and on it went.

Elliott fiddled with the data on his screens. He glanced at me. "Rough night, kid?"

"The new hours," I explained, though I knew that was only half the story, "I'm not used to it."

He stared at my get up. "You sleep in those?"

I looked at myself. I had forgotten to change clothes from the first half of the day. "Sort of."

A couple of hours later, I started to smell. I called Emily around three a.m., woke her, and asked her to bring me fresh clothes and deodorant in the morning.

"I don't know," she said.

"Please. Please."

"I feel like a laundry service."

Emily worked in fashion. She loved clothes. "You've got great taste, pick something—I don't know, brash."

"You don't own anything brash."

"When you get up."

"I'm up now."

"Please. Before the day-people arrive. Six o'clock. Can you be here at six?"

I heard her yawn. "You know this is kind of messed up."

I knew she'd make it. At six, I snuck off and changed into a fresh Brooks Brothers shirt—light blue, with a pear green and rose pink tattersall pattern, a light green Vineyard Vines tie with baby blue parachutes scattered across to match—and cleaned up in the bathroom. I washed my face and threw water in my hair, then used eye drops to freshen my star-glazed eyeballs. Boom. Only six hours to go.

I made it. It wasn't pretty, but I did.

Elliott finished his day looking chipper as ever. He said, "Hey, kid. Let's go get a beer." A quick stop in the bathroom and a single line of cocaine, and that's just what I did.

I drove back to Villanova in the fall for the start of my senior year, partied for a week, then on a lark, drove two hours north for no other reason than to get high with Derek up in Montville. When I got to his house, Derek was mixing a drink. "You have to try this."

On the counter was a tall Styrofoam cup and next to it a little brown bottle with a white and red and green label. "Is that cough syrup?" I asked.

"No, well yeah. Promethazine. With codeine in it. Prescription. Wait, here's the secret ingredient." He opened the fridge and grabbed a bottle of Sprite, poured it into the glass, over ice, then snatched up the cough syrup and dumped about a third of the bottle on top of the Sprite. It fizzed and made a red mess.

"I've heard of this before and always wanted to try it."

Derek looked at me and frowned. "You ever hear of Lil Wayne?"

Ignoring his sarcasm, I said, "So, you drink it."

"*We* drink it." He lifted the glass in a mock toast, said, "There you have it, my new recreational drug. Thank you, Hi-Tech." I learned later Hi-Tech was the maker of the cough syrup.

He took a sip and I watched him, waiting for a reaction, but all I saw was a timid smile. I said, "Let me try."

He handed me the Styrofoam cup. "Sip it. Go slow."

Promethazine with codeine cough syrup mongered the nickname *lean* for the effects it causes on users after consumption. The enormous amounts of opiate and antihistamines cause the user to naturally lean back or sway due to the high it produces. It was like a pill in liquid form. The biggest difference? It tasted delicious.

Hi-Tech was nicknamed "sweet red," due to the reddish tint of the cough syrup, and the candy-like sweet taste of the syrup. I bought a few ounces of the syrup and grabbed my own soda to mix together. I took the pharmacy bottle full of cough syrup and poured it into the soda. It looked like a lava lamp, the way the syrup swam all the way down to the bottom of the soda bottle. It looked the same when you mixed olive oil and water together.

I slowly turned the bottle upside down and continued to flip it back and forth until the soda and the cough syrup blended and became one beautiful red mixture.

So there I was, sipping lean for most of the night, smoking pot, and I think I did one, maybe two little blue pills.

I had arrived in Montville around six that evening, sipped and smoked and snorted for the next four hours, a continuous evening of chemical intake, and then I stood, a little shaky, and declared I was heading down to Villanova. I'd made the drive so many times, I could do it in my sleep.

Derek said, "Stay the night."

"I'm all right."

"Stay."

"I have classes, early. I'm okay, really."

"Don't be a college boy. Stay. Pass out. I got a couch and a spare bed, if you want it."

I was high. I was stupid. I said no.

Sometime after ten, I climbed in my Cherokee, found I-287 after a couple of tries, and aimed south. Then I got tired. And more tired. I nodded off, caught myself, nodded off again. My head rocked forward and woke me. I exited, listened to my GPS, made a right, all on autopilot. My ears and hands and feet knew what to do, even if my head wasn't working too well. Forty-five minutes into the trip, I nodded off a couple of more times, then my body gave up, and I passed out. That's when I hit the car.

It was a big car—American, green, dead still at a stoplight.

I was doing sixty, so the police report said.

I smashed into the car in front of me, who smashed into the car in front of it and pushed this other car, innocent of all wrongdoing, into the intersection where it sat motionless until the police arrived.

My airbag hit me in the face and probably saved my life. And more importantly, it woke me. I still had some goddamn lean with me. Before I left Derek's, I'd upended the Hi-Tech bottle into whatever was left in the bottle of Sprite. I got out of my poor Cherokee, dumped the red gunk from the Sprite bottle, and tossed the bottle next to the road.

I still had the 16-ounce-bottle of Hi-Tech, maybe 2 ounces left, so I locked the syrup, baggie of blues, and some pot in the glove compartment. I tidied up my Jeep, so it looked nice when the cops arrived, and not long after a polite EMT all but forced me to ride with him to Robert Wood Johnson University Hospital in Somerville for a little look-see. My chest hurt. And my knees. Better to be safe, the guy said.

Before I left the scene, a tall police officer talked to me, hinted that I was on my phone at the time, maybe jacking with the GPS, making a call, texting. He was fishing, and I gave him a look of guilt, glanced down and to the side, no eye contact. That's all he needed to conclude I was a well-meaning shitbag college kid on his phone, and not a junkie sipping lean while operating heavy machinery at sixty mph.

The good doctors at Robert Wood Johnson got me checked out. Bruises, rightfully pissed off bystanders, nothing more.

I stood out on the curb, waiting for the car service to haul me back to Villanova. I had one problem. All my pharmaceuticals were locked in my glove compartment. Fuck. I had an hour or more on the road to come up with a plan. Here it was. I'd get back to the house in Bryn Mawr, borrow a car from a buddy—not Fitzy—meet up with Meech in Philly and pick up some pills. It was a good plan.

Well thought out.

Doable.

A few days later, I drove in a rental car to the wrecking yard in Somerville, took some pics of my murdered Grand Cherokee, and grabbed a few things I didn't care about along with my syrup, pills, and pot from my glove box, which I did care about.

I hurried to the nearest 7-Eleven, grabbed a bottle of Sprite, poured in the last of my Hi-Tech, and sipped away as I drove attentively back to Bryn Mawr.

The next day, I rented a Chevy pickup truck. I'd always wanted a truck, and the agency had a black Silverado with big tires. What the hell, right? But I hadn't driven a large truck in a while, and I'd forgotten how difficult it was to see out the rearview mirror. A week later, I backed into a Wells Fargo ATM machine, didn't stop, and rammed a parked taxi with the ass end of my rented Silverado. The taxi driver got out, surprised and a little angry, started walking my way, when I sped off.

I was meeting Meech in Philly. I had business to take care of.

Not ten goddamn minutes later, I was at a red light minding my own goddamn business. The light changed, I started my turn, and a crappy little white Toyota hit me head-on. My already dented Silverado was now toast.

The other driver was large and stuck. He hit me so hard his doors folded in on themselves. One window worked, and before the police or fire department arrived, another car dropped by, three dudes and a woman. The woman got out, crying, screaming, reached through the window into the back seat and pulled out a baby. No way that baby was strapped into a car seat. She and the baby got in the other car and zoomed away.

When the firefighters appeared, they cut the driver out and found some weed in the car. I overheard someone say he smelled of alcohol. *Reeked* was the word I heard.

None of it my fault. Wrong place. Wrong time. I was inno-cent. This time.

I know how that sounds, given everything I had done, but I was doing a good job of suppressing any guilt...or at least trying to.

Then a police officer pulled me aside, said he had a report that my SUV had been involved in a hit and run. A taxi, not long ago. The officer walked slowly to the rear of the Silverado and examined the bumper. He said, "You have any idea the trouble people get in for leaving the scene of an accident?"

"Okay, okay," I said. "It was me."

The office spoke slowly, in no rush. "I know it was you. You want to tell me why?"

"A week ago I was involved in an accident." I glanced at my smashed Silverado. "I got scared. I know I shouldn't have driven away. It was wrong, I know it." I shook my head like I couldn't believe it. "Then I back into a taxi. Now this."

The officer tilted his head, thinking. "The way I see it, this wasn't your fault. As for the other...I'll write you a ticket, you pay a fine. Do me a favor and don't do it again."

Afterwards, I called a fraternity friend who promised to pick me up. Before he arrived, I phoned Meech, told him I'd been delayed (here I sounded really put out), and asked if we could meet up tomorrow.

"I'm standing right here," he said.

"Ah, man."

"Right now. I'm fucking waiting. When was the last time you seen me wait? I'm across the street. In front of the big iron-col-ored building."

"I'm sorry, really. See, I got into an accident—"

"You think I need a story? Did I ask for a story?"

"It wasn't my fault man."

"What did you just say?"

"He hit *me*."

This went on for a bit, Meech laying into me, me groveling. Then he hung up on me.

I thought of my father in that moment, when he was my age. He worked three jobs throughout college. Here I was wrecking an expensive car that I didn't pay for, regularly skipping classes, and barely getting through a cushy internship in between lines of cocaine and pills and otherwise doing a shitty job of holding up the Bocchi name.

12

My senior year at Villanova, I kept to myself. Couldn't risk people seeing me *get* high. I spent hours locked in my room, on my bed, laying there euphoric and drugged, my body dissolving into the Tempur-Pedic memory foam. Sometimes when I was doped, I'd grab my MacBook Pro and search through 9/11 videos. If I found something new, I'd watch it over and over. Airliners crashing into the towers, people jumping, buildings collapsing. At some point, say after a hundred views, I'd go numb. Then I wanted to forget. So I'd do more drugs.

In early December, my buddy Louie walked into my room with a bottle of Jack Daniels in his hand. I could smell booze on his breath, thick and acidic. Louie was a good guy—difficult past and easy to anger, but a good guy nonetheless. He loved conspiracy theories, especially those involving 9/11. His favorite theme was that the government did it, likely set the whole thing in motion, if not directly, then in ways Louie could never put his finger on.

When it came to any talk of 9/11, most of my friends walked on eggshells. Why mouth off if it might hurt feelings or end with a punch in the nose? Louie, on the other hand, was a man without filters.

"Boch," he said, "What you got there?"

I had a Swisher Sweet cigarillo in my lap. I cut open the cigarillo and dumped out the tobacco and filled it with weed. Rolled it back up, and she was ready to go.

Louie took a step closer to the nightstand, leaned forward to put the bottle of Jack on the low table, then changed his mind. "Have a swig." Louie was weaving, drunk, hammered, the bottle in his hand wobbling back and forth.

"Give me that," I said.

Louie glanced around the room, at the television. "Turn it on."

I grabbed the remote. "Sports?"

"Shit no. Cartoons."

We drank and smoked and watched cartoons. It was nice, like being six years old all over again. No worries. No responsibilities. On-screen, a crudely drawn building blew up.

"I'm curious," Louie said.

"What?"

"Don't get mad."

"What?"

"Did they ever find your dad?"

"Why do you want to know?" I asked.

"I already said. I'm curious."

I hesitated for a moment. I was loopy, kind of fuzzy in my thinking. "They found most of him."

"Oh man."

What now? I thought to myself. I really didn't care what he was about to say. I had zero desire to have this conversation, let alone with Louie.

"In some of the videos," Louie continued, "you can see evidence of thermite."

"I'm not in the mood."

"Lots of molten metal. Photographs, eyewitnesses, all kinds of proof. Had to be explosives in the buildings, in the rubble. No other explanation."

"Dude, I really don't fucking care how the towers came down. They came down. That's all that matters to me."

Louie kept his mouth shut for ten seconds, then said, "That shit was in the ground for months after the attack."

I stood, just to be doing something. "Doesn't change a thing."

Truth was, some days I believed the theories—the government was involved, high-level officials got an advance warning, and the big one, the whole fucking mess was a controlled demolition and not a structural failure. Other days, I didn't.

Louie stared at the TV, his back to me, said, "The government's got these big-ass cameras in the sky. They showed the temperature on the ground, different spots, too fucking hot for a structure fire."

"Louie, take your bottle and go fuck yourself."

In December, southeastern Pennsylvania got hit hard with snow, so bad the people in charge told everyone to stay inside, state of emergency, give the plows a chance to clear the streets. I needed money, and I needed drugs in that order.

I called my mother and asked, "How are you?"

"Joe just finished plowing. Lots of snow here. You?"

"We just shoveled." I sat in the dark, a couple of candles on the coffee table. After all that shoveling, my roommates were scattered around the house, lighting up candles and joints in the basement, trying to warm up.

"You're not driving anywhere. Don't drive. Please."

"We lost power at the house," I said. "We were thinking of getting a hotel. Can you send me six hundred? Might be a couple of nights. Plus food and stuff."

"Sure. Please, let me know when you get there. I worry about you."

We did lose power at The Brick, but all fourteen of us planned to stick it out, stay inside and light a shitload of candles and get drunk and stoned. A handful of guys talked of snorting cocaine. I didn't care about that stuff. I needed pills.

I called Meech. "What's good?" I asked.

"You know. Jawns all around."

"Thirty," I said.

"And Zs?"

"Ten for now."

"I got you."

I glanced out the front window, snow falling sideways, piling up on the porch I just shoveled. "I'm coming through," I said. "Be patient. It's shitty out."

I was already stoned, kind of droopy-eyed. I bundled up and walked out to my car parked at the curb, the fresh snow from last night at least a foot deep on the road and way deeper in places. It was unsafe to drive. No shit. Not a car moving on our street.

I was too lazy to scrape the windshield. My Rover had a heated windshield. A little heat, a little wipers, I'd be fine. I climbed in, turned the ignition, and flipped the wipers. *Snap.* The left windshield wiper shattered. Either I was higher than I thought or dumber. I turned off the wipers, gave the windshield some time to thaw, and then tried it again. The passenger's side worked okay. I was too cold to do anything about the broken wiper, so I left the pieces where they were, a stick-like arm scraping the windshield at a steady pace.

The snow was pressed flat against the road in the center, sort of ice cubey and piled high at the edges. My Land Rover had four-wheel drive. I would be fine.

It took me a while to get to Philly. This time I had the snow to blame. If I didn't get more meds, I'd face withdrawal soon. Locked up with thirteen other dudes, all drinking and having fun, and me with tremors and diarrhea.

My cell phone vibrated. "Where you at?" Meech said.

"I'm close. It's fucking awful out. I'm coming."

"East Allegheny Avenue and Collins Street," he said. "Not the other."

We switched drop sites in the winter, no telling why. "I know the address. It's fucking snowing."

"I'm out here in the cold and you yelling at me?"

"Not what I meant. See you soon."

I drove and my Rover fishtailed. I sped up and slowed down. Turned into the slide and turned the other way. None of it made much difference. I'd get there faster if I crawled.

I tooled up East Allegheny Avenue then over some other street or alley and back down Collins Street, a one-way. A bunch of abandoned warehouses on my right, a Sunoco gas station up ahead. I drove like an old lady, hunched over, hands knuckly-white gripping the wheel, thinking I should have sprung for the heated steering wheel, and I skidded into a goddamned parked car. *Clunk.* The guy was right there, not in the car but appearing beside it. A dark brown face in a mountain of clothing, jackets, a hat, and some old scarf wrapped around his neck.

I thought, I'm about to get mugged. In a Philadelphia snowstorm. I pulled out my cash, held onto a hundred, and put the rest in the glove box and locked it.

I backed up, put the Rover in park right there in the middle of the street, left it running, and got out. Clearly, I had no place being in Philly in the middle of a snowstorm, let alone a state of emergency. Yet here I was, the typical privileged white college kid, scoring drugs in the hood when I should be in my cushy apartment watching TV or something. The look of disdain was apparent on the guy's face, but it lightened up at the thought of a quick buck.

"I'm sorry. Really. The snow. I've got four-wheel drive, for all the good it does. I probably paid extra, and when you need it, well..." I was rambling, semi-stoned, standing in South Philly freezing my ass off talking to a bundle of clothing and a big round face.

I looked at his car, frowning as if really studying the damage. He stared more or less in the same location. It was hard to tell the make with all the snow, something old. Hard to see much of anything. Could be nothing under all that dirt and snow. Could be a sizable dent. I said, "What do you think?"

"You mean should we call a cop?"

"In this weather?" I looked up, snow falling on my face.

He thought for a moment, rewrapped the knitted thing round his neck, green and gray. Ah, a Philadelphia Eagles scarf. He said, "What *did* you mean?"

"I meant how much?"

"Oh," he said, a big smile showing, way ahead of me.

"Will forty cover it?" I had the money in my hand.

"I do believe sixty would."

I handed him three twenties—part of my drug stash.

"Thanks, again," I said. "I mean, sorry." I didn't know what I was saying. Then I waved and got back in my SUV.

I drove slow. Real slow. Crawled along until I saw Meech standing next to a building. He came to me, clapping his hands together, head down, cussing under his breath, tossed my pills through my open window into the passenger seat. I handed him the money. He pulled his puffy hoodie tighter around his face and jogged away. Not a word.

I didn't move. I looked at the baggie of pills beside me, felt pretty good about that. Got into another accident, but—and this is a big but—I got myself out of it. Felt pretty good about that. I put both hands on the wheel, stared out the windshield, the snow coming down like a blanket of goose down, the same shit in Meech's North Face puffy jacket. My window was open and the neighborhood was quiet—free of all commotion besides the snow circulating in the air. It was quieter than I'd ever heard it. And I felt pretty good about that.

I texted my mother. *Made it to hotel. All safe.*

Thank you for letting me know, she responded.

Farrell says thank you for the room. My part, anyway.

You're welcome. Be good.

I typed, *I'll call soon. Love you.*

I love you too.

13

BEFORE MY MOM AND JOE and brothers and relatives drove down for my graduation ceremony, I treated myself to my final Villanova buy—one hundred blue pills, thirty xannie bars, and 8 ounces of prescription cough syrup. This was a final exam I knew I could ace.

I was solid for the festivities.

Which might explain why I was late.

I slept in. When I woke up, I knew I couldn't drive to campus and find parking, and was way too lazy for the twelve-minute jog. I finally called my brother Nick to come get me. Nick didn't know the area and his GPS sent him to the country club where we spent the night before. Thirty minutes later he showed up, we rushed to The Pavilion, and I strolled in half-high, wearing a day-old shirt and tie, khakis, cap and gown, all of it a wrinkled mess.

I got a bunch of money for graduation, close to six thousand dollars from aunts and uncles, extended families on both sides, and even Joe's family pitched in.

I spent all of it on pills. Every cent.

My mom gave me one of my dad's hard-earned Rolex watches as my graduation gift.

A month after arriving back home in New Vernon, I was broke. I did a little dealing, and when things really got tight, I extorted money from anyone nearby.

My mother was closest.

I drove to meet a dealer in Hillside, pulled into a Bed Bath & Beyond, and parked. I had a scheme rumbling around inside my head, this one to hit up my mother for two, three thousand dollars. To buy a camera, I'd tell her. When she asked to see the camera, I'd think of something, maybe rent one for a couple of months, a place I'd found online, BorrowLenses, one-fifty a month, and when she lost interest, return the rental. I had my pitch all thought out.

I called and gave her my spiel. She wasn't buying.

I called again, came at it a different way, more emotional, *I need help* with a beggy tone to my voice.

I called again, this time said I wanted to freelance, maybe start a small business. I loved photography—I'd found my passion in life. As it happened, I bought my first camera about the time I went to college and was always taking pictures at Villanova and home. Eventually, I sold the camera but kept some of the lenses. The passion thing wasn't so far-fetched. She didn't buy it.

Still sitting in my Rover in the BB&B parking lot, I dialed, one last time, said, "I know we talked about this, but I need the money."

"You need to get a job," she said.

"Just twenty-five hundred," I said. "This is a Nikon D700, I told you that before. It sounds like a lot, but it's not. Really, this guy is giving me a hell of a deal. I don't know what it runs full retail, but it's a lot."

"Matthew, do you know how many times you've called me in the last two hours?"

"Twelve point one megapixels," I said. "FX format, you know what that is? And these special sensors, so much stuff I don't know what all it does. Mom, this is the one. You know me, I've done the research."

"I don't think spending three thousand dollars for a camera is a smart idea."

I was flustered, angry, not nearly high enough for this conversation. I half-shouted, "This is stupid."

"Which part—you calling every twenty minutes or you refusing to get a job?"

"Mom."

"Honey, you've spent a month in your room. Don't you think it's time?"

"With the photography I can freelance, make some money while I look. It's not that easy. The job market, it's, you know. A trading desk, those are not everyday jobs. Equity sales, trading, I'm open to the right position. You know that. It's hard...read the papers."

"Have you even tried?"

"Yeah, I've fucking tried. You've no idea how hard it is to get a job on Wall Street. Look," I said, "I really want this. It's important to me. What do you say?" Pause. "And I'll quit calling."

Here she took a breath, inhaled loud enough for me to hear. "Joe and I talked."

"Mom."

"I want you to listen to this. *We* don't think it's a good idea to give you money like this. It feels like it never ends. Is there an end? I love you, you know that."

"Mom, look..." But that's all I had.

"I have to go. Matthew, this is no fun for me. You understand how stressful this is? Do you? Because I don't think you do."

"Two thousand three hundred. I might be able to get him down."

"I'm hanging up."

"Wait, wait, what am I supposed to do?"

She was exasperated, her voice dry and throaty. "Talk to your uncle Frank," she said, and she hung up on me.

Before he died, my father set up investment accounts for us boys—cash accounts used to wire money. After he died, there were trust accounts set up, with stocks and bonds and other assets. I sort of had access to the cash account, with approval. No way I had access to the trust accounts, or I'd have bled them dry long ago.

My uncle Frank, my mother's cousin, was now a co-trustee, along with my mother, of the accounts. In his youth, Frank put in twenty-five years with a bullish financial services firm, FVP, as the Managing Director of Investments, before starting a sustainable water grid infrastructure company in New York City. The man was no slouch, and he stood between me and my money. I mean me and my oxy, whatever.

Submit a wire request by four p.m. and I'd have the money today. After, and I was screwed. For Frank, I'd have to put on a performance, a masterpiece of manipulation, and I had to start the charade now.

I called him. "Uncle Frank, I really need the money today for the camera."

"Matthew, how are you? Doing well, I hope."

"Yeah, thank you for asking. The camera, it's an investment, really—"

"Your mother mentioned it."

"Special order," I said. "It's just what I need."

"I see," he said.

This was taking too long. Frank was a thinker, a logician. I needed a cut-the-check-and-get-out-of-my-face guy.

I said, "I'll freelance. Just until I land a trading gig in the City."

"I am thrilled to hear you want to make some money while looking for more permanent work." He paused so long I didn't know if it was my turn. When I started to speak, he said, "I talked with your mother not long ago. We agreed it's a lot of money you're asking for. Would you agree?"

"That it's a lot of money? No, well, not really. No. It's a high-end camera...is that what you mean?"

"I need you to send me a business proposal. Your freelance projections, I'd like to see them on paper. Income per shoot, that sort of thing."

"A report?"

"A proposal. Nothing extensive. Look, even if you send it soon, I make no guarantees we can do anything today."

I started to think the man could see through my bullshit.

I said, "I'm not home. How about I send you the document, the proposal, when I get home?"

"Entirely up to you."

"If you could approve the wire now, it'd really help."

"I'd sure like a look at the proposal."

"Of course. I understand."

I glanced at the time. I was anxious, sweaty, on the verge of an emotional outburst or two.

"Listen, Matthew. I told your mother, I see my role as your *consigliere*. Your counselor. *The Godfather*, you remember the movie. Imagine you are Michael. I am Tom."

"Well, sure."

"I'm *your* financial counselor; however, I oversee these accounts for your *father*. My aim is to ensure his legacy is spent the way he wanted it spent. You understand what I'm saying to you?"

The art of the stall, I understand that. Besides, how does anyone know my father didn't want his legacy spent on oxy and Xanax?

But just the mention of my father brought tears. Real tears and a break in my voice—something I could use to my advantage. "He would want that," I said. "Your guidance, I mean."

"Yes, yes he would." In the background, I heard papers shuffling. "I'm worried, however. Can I speak freely, just between you and me?"

I sniffled loudly into the phone. I was teary-eyed, but I had it together. "Go on."

"It's my guess that you are using drugs again. Don't say anything. I don't want to start an argument. My point, I believe the drugs are clouding your judgment."

"I don't know what to say."

"Tell me, Matthew, is there any truth to what I'm saying?"

Frank had a way of listening, or *not* talking—a man comfortable in silence, and he hit me with it now. This long, dead lull.

"Well," I said. "I'm not sure what you're saying. I understand the words, but, ask me again."

"Are you using?" He spoke slow, stretching out each give and take. "It's a simple question."

"No," I said. "Some pot is all. Just some, not a lot." Then something let go. I started bawling. I mean real goddamn tears this time. Every once in a while, I'd let out a sort of hiccup, an involuntary cry-baby hiccup. No way could I fake this. It just came out of me. I said, "I am not doing pills." *Sob. Sob. Hiccup.* "I can tell you that, no pills."

This was the performance of a lifetime. I was good at this, way better than I thought. The tears, wherever they came from, were a stroke of genius. Some part of me knew I needed tears, real snot-inducing tears and hiccups and the bellyacher grimace on my face, which I suspected jumped through the phone line. I needed all of it to pull this off, and goddamn, it all came together.

I had him.

"Send me something, a page or so," he said. "As soon as you can, and we can discuss it further."

Fuck.

I looked at my watch, a quarter past four.

My uncle Frank had beaten me, bested me at my own game, and deep down, I think he knew it.

I texted my mom, told her I'd spoken to Frank. Said I'd put together a proposal. A lie that never happened.

On the fly, I came up with another lie—some plausible rationale for her extending me money, just a few hundred dollars, but enough to get me through the day. My drug habit was tenacious, overpowering, though I didn't think of it that way. I didn't think of it in any comprehensive way. I simply woke up, got out of bed, and wondered where to get my next handful of pills. One day at a time. Today, I needed money. I used the money to buy pills. Today. This wasn't a grand scheme I was plotting. Just a kid, a college grad no less, trying to make it through the day without muscle aches, and tearing up, and a runny nose, and agitation, an inkling of depression. In other words, without a hint of withdrawal.

You're relentless, my mother texted.

I love you, I typed. *Thank you.*

14

I SHOWED UP TO JACK'S graduation party semi-put together, nearly an hour late—not bad given my tendency to lose track of time. Jack was one of my best friends from Nova but lived close to me in Jersey.

The party was elegant, decorated, five-star hors d'oeuvres, a dinner after, open bar.

Jack's family house looked like it belonged in Greece, columns and fluting holding up elaborate cornice-work. The pool house was more of the same, itself large enough to house a family of six. An hour in, I was nearly incoherent on blues, xannie bars, booze, and weed. I had some cocaine with me, so I ambled out back to the pool house, into one of the bathrooms—exposed rock on the floor and bluish sandy walls—and snorted a line. I needed a pick-me-up bad to keep from nodding—a noticeable sign I'd had too much, an involuntary drifting, a here one moment and gone the next feeling. On the outside, nodding looked like the guy across the table—me—had momentarily passed out, and a millisecond later lurched back to life.

Nodding at one of your best friend's grad party wasn't cool.

Back inside the big house, someone suggested we start chugging beers, so we did.

Next, we ripped a few shots of Patron. Then another shot for good measure.

After the beers and shots, I snuck off to the bathroom and inhaled another line of cocaine.

Without the coke, I'd crash.

I stood there in the bathroom, suddenly awestruck by this opulent marble countertop, recrystallized rock, this vibrant yellow and violet, dug up over there I think someone said, Kozani or some such place, and I just stood there staring, a little white line of cocaine powder against the yellow stone and I took it all in. I was lunatic high, of course, and for a moment, I felt like that guy in the movie *The Wolf of Wall Street,* Jordan Belfort, made thousands of dollars a minute trading and spent it on drugs and sex and globe-trotting. My job at ACM started in a couple weeks. Archibald Capital Management, financial services, a powerhouse bank in Germany, me nestled in the Midtown Manhattan office. I, too, could make lots of money and blow it on drugs and sex and travel. I was a little Jordan Belfort in the making.

Then I looked at myself in the mirror. I was pasty-faced, white and doughy, with dark circles under my eyes. I'd gone fat. Blues and xannie bars tinkered with my metabolism. The blues made me constipated, while the xannies and weed-smoking made me hungry, no, *ravenous.* I was taking in great gobs of food and couldn't shit, or at least shit out all I'd taken in. Each day for the last four years, I'd gotten bigger. The change was so slow, I didn't notice. I arrived at Villanova University, a slim one-forty, came away nearly two hundred pounds, all of it walrus blubber. Now, here I was at a flashy graduation party, all my friends as trim as Aspens and I looked past the marble countertop, and there I was, this pale, roly-poly person I never wanted to be.

Fuck.

I snorted a line of cocaine, and it all went away.

After dinner, we opened several bottles of Pinot noir, sipped, sipped, then I eased off to my favorite bathroom and fingered a dinky Xanax bar out of my mini baggie, broke it into pieces along the scored lines, swallowed three-quarters, then crushed and snorted the last quarter—my go-to move. Later, I returned and crushed and snorted another four blues.

It was a long way to morning, and I didn't want to be stranded without pills, so I brought with me thirty blue pills, five xannie bars, an eight ball of cocaine, and a quarter ounce of weed. All for this one night. By now, I could do thirty oxycodone and ten Xanax in a day. It was work, but I could do it.

I strolled into the kitchen. Hungry, even though the tuna tartare and avocado mousse from dinner were somewhere in my small intestine. I looked through the kitchen cabinets for something sweet. I started at one end and moved right, opening every cabinet door on the way. One of the cabinets was filled with prescription drugs.

I was so excited I wanted to tell someone.

I couldn't, of course, but I wanted to.

I came across a 10-ounce bottle of Hi-Tech promethazine with codeine cough syrup. My favorite brand of lean and pricey— fifty dollars an ounce.

I judged the bottle, which had about 3.5 ounces left—enough for a nice, dreamy high.

I poured the remnants of the Hi-Tech syrup into an empty plastic water bottle and replaced the Hi-Tech with NyQuil, also in the cabinet. Who'd know?

I gripped the water bottle, now filled with red gunk, ambled out of the kitchen, across the noisy hardwood hallway—mahogany with a Greek key motif at the edges—and out the front door where I hid the bottle in my car. I returned, put on a face, told Jack I wasn't feeling well, and I was heading home. I drove straight to 7-Eleven, bought a bottle of Sprite, and poured my 3.5 ounces into the bottle of soda. Next stop was my room, where I spent the evening all by my lonesome. Just me and sweet red.

In July, I was obliged to attend a one-week family trip to Jamaica, Montego Bay. Well in advance of takeoff, I invested six grand in a little travel booty—180 oxycodone pills and thirty-five Xanax bars—my seven-day cache of pharmaceuticals. Jamaica was all right. In some ways, just another Caribbean island with lush topography and rainforests and reef-lined beaches.

I tried to spread out my oxy intake, four blues every four hours. A Xanax every six. Mix in some cocaine I'd buy off strangers on the beach, and I was set.

My habit was four blues before dinner. When no one was looking, I'd slip into the bathroom, turn on the shower, and do my thing. On day three, I walked out of the bathroom into the main room, and Nick was standing there next to my mother. He said, "Nice nose."

I hadn't double-checked myself in the mirror—a rookie move. I brushed the blue dust away with my hand.

My mother said, "You snorted something."

"What? No."

"What was it?"

"No," I said. "I mean, nothing." I was half-baked, high enough I wasn't making any sense, a kind of perpetual state I'd gotten used to and was sort of surprised everyone else wasn't used to it.

Mom was pissed. "In the bathroom, you put something up your nose. What was it?"

"Okay, okay. Adderall. Jeez, I don't know why this is anyone's business." I even had a prescription for the stuff.

"You snorted Adderall? This is something people do?"

Ah, yes. Snort the stuff and it's absorbed within minutes, hits the blood-brain barrier faster than you can change the channel. I nodded dumbly.

My mother pointed at me but didn't speak. After a moment, she marched off to the kitchen.

Nick laughed.

Michael, who hadn't been paying attention, just shook his head.

Everyone knew I was lying. I couldn't give two shits. I was high, and life was good.

That night after dinner, I went outside onto the hotel balcony. I had a couple of beers with me. Drank, smoked a couple of joints. Blew smoke into the air and watched it float over the balcony railing.

Nick showed up, slid the large balcony doors shut behind him. He had his laptop with him. Opened the lid and started surfing. By now, Nick was doing his own 9/11 research. He didn't care about jumpers, how fast they fell, what they looked like after an awkward landing. He was more concerned with cause and effect. Who was behind it all? Why now? How exactly did such a massive structure come straight down upon itself?

Nick wanted verifiable facts, but when the facts lacked a certain mystery or daring, he'd settle for a conspiracy.

He said, "Says here that traders knew it was coming."

"Traders?"

"Right before the attacks, a bunch of traders, well...I don't know if it was a bunch, but a few anyway, they shorted United Airlines stock."

"Wall Street types brought down the towers," I said. "Is that it?"

"And American Airlines. It's what it says."

I pushed a freshly lit joint his way. "You want some of this?"

Nick glanced over his shoulder into the hotel room. "Not right now. Are you even listening?"

"What else?" I asked.

"The terrorists' passports, some other ID-type shit was found. You believe that? How does a bunch of paper survive an explosion like that?"

"Has to be a conspiracy, is what you're saying?"

"Has to be."

Nick and I were close, but when it came to 9/11, to our father's death, we didn't connect. "Be right back," I said.

The conversation made me think too much. Lucky me, I knew a shortcut to quash that shit. I stood and darted inside. In the bathroom, I snorted four blues, swallowed two xannies. Didn't take three minutes. This put me at four blues over my daily recommended dosage. I stumbled out to the balcony and fell onto the lounge chair.

Nick glanced at me, shook his head, said I looked like shit. Then he started in on the assassination of JFK, for godsakes. The blues kicked in—or was it the xannies?—whichever. I was tired and high and half-sloshed. I couldn't keep my eyes open. I started nodding, my eyelids hovering sort of mid-eyeball, the muscles in my neck going rubbery, my head seesawing like a life-sized bobblehead.

"Hey, Matt," Nick said, his voice raised. "Wake up."

"I'm awake."

"You're fucked up."

"Am not."

"You are, dude," he said, and that's the last thing I remember.

When we returned, I started work at ACM. I was the newest junior analyst responsible for researching stocks and bonds. Not a particularly difficult job, really. Not after I got the hang of it.

I started off at Villanova in the business school, but eventually switched to liberal arts in pursuit of something that made me truly happy. I enjoyed going on service trips in high school and college and loved the experiences of helping people in need, so I wanted to go into a field where I could continue to do that. Uncle Tony told me it was a big mistake to switch, but I did it anyway. But by the end of college, I decided I wanted to follow in my father's footsteps and go into finance. I wanted to keep his legacy alive and make him proud, and this was the only way I knew how. I also wanted to make a lot of money and be rich enough to buy whatever I wanted—in reality, more drugs.

I told myself that I was going to keep his legacy alive each day by wearing that Rolex watch and eventually make a name for myself on Wall Street. I would work my way up like he did, although on a much easier path. But nonetheless, I would become successful, even more successful than he was, running a major financial empire or something. That would make him proud. The drugs part of this Jordan Belfort picture, on the other hand, wouldn't.

The start of a new job was the perfect time to stop with all the painkillers and benzos and coke.

Couldn't do it.

And truthfully, I didn't want to do it.

I envisioned for myself a high rise apartment in Manhattan, a *Great Gatsby*-esque house in the burbs, the finest sports cars, a smoking hot wife. And of course, a shit ton of pills and cocaine that I could consume on a daily basis.

As a thank you to my higher-ups at ACM, I showed up to work late. Every day. I made excuse after excuse until no one bothered asking.

I still sourced my prescriptions one day at a time. My plan, if you could call it that, was to get pills the night before. After work each day, I'd head to Newark, buy enough meds for the next day. On rare occasions, if I didn't have enough to get me through the workday, I contacted my NYC delivery service guy. He got me what I needed. Double the price, but he always came through.

Early on, I was asked to stay late after the market closed. Stick close to the trading desk, and when my boss Gabe called, give him an update on the day's events. Couldn't be easier, happy to do it.

Then my Midtown delivery guy, Jose called. "It's me. I'm at East Forty-Eighth and Madison Avenue."

"I'm at the office."

"You got the cash?"

"In my pocket."

Jose was Spanish or Mexican, Guatemalan maybe, heavy, favored designer belts and nice jeans and Gucci tee shirts. Bathed in cologne. He said, "Then get a move on."

I *really* needed my shit. "I've got a thing at the office. I'm stuck, any way you can come to me?"

He was eating or drinking, something slurpy and nasty sounding. He said, "Can't. I'm running late. It's Madison or nothing. Hurry, I got to piss."

ACM was a couple of blocks west on Sixth Avenue. I could get there and back in ten, fifteen minutes. Assuming no delays.

I said, "I'm coming."

I hustled east on 48th, passed Mendy's Kosher Delicatessen and Citibank and Bank of China, lots of banks, in my Brooks Brothers two-button suit and Vineyard Vines tie, yellow with tiny buildings and bridges on it. It was July and hot. I was sweating. I finally saw Jose's car just around the corner, a white Audi R8, tinted windows, blacked-out rims. I crawled inside. The cologne hit me hard.

"I gotta take a piss," he said.

"I'm kind of in a hurry."

He was already out the door. "Be right back." Where he was going, who knew, maybe a Starbucks.

Five minutes later, I got a call from a guy at the office that Gabe wanted to know where I was. Then Gabe himself called, and I let it go to voicemail. Then they both called, and I didn't answer either. What could I say?

Fifteen goddamn minutes later, Jose strolled up to the car. I got my drugs and sprinted back to the office, called Gabe, a real dick of a human being who wore fucking ugly Hermés ties, a guy with more money than, oh, I don't know, Leno? And I listened to him berate the new kid, *me*, for a solid twenty minutes because

I was late to a phone call. According to Gabe, I had zero dedication, even less drive, a bucket full of selfishness, and I didn't know what else.

Dick.

If the blues and xannies didn't kill me, the monotony would.

I would wake up every day at five-thirty or six in the morning. I didn't wake up to an alarm, but rather when my withdrawal symptoms would cause me to turn over and grab some pills from my nightstand to snort in order to start the day. Most of the time, I woke to my mom screaming at me since I overslept again. If I had any leftover coke, I would do a few lines to give me even more of a jump start on the day and then enjoy a nice Marlboro 27 cigarette with my Dunkin' Donuts iced coffee. Once I got to the office, I would begin the day researching whatever Gabe demanded I look into but would be too distracted trying to figure out how to get enough money in order to buy the next large quantity of pills. This went on day after day.

By late September, a couple of months on the job, I had settled into a pattern.

At the end of each day, I walked fifteen long-ass blocks deeper into Midtown, caught the train at Penn Station, West Thirty-Third and Seventh Avenue. Took the Dover Line, due west, to Madison, New Jersey, an hour flat. Got in my Rover, drove back the way I'd just come, thirty minutes east, to Newark where I met Dre, my connection, and where I gave up all my cash in exchange for a handful of silly blue pills. But my routine was not over yet. I climbed back in my Rover, did yet another one-eighty, headed west this time for another forty-minute drive home. Safe and sound.

Smoke some weed, snort some blues, pop some xannies.

Sleep.

Get up tomorrow, and do it all over again.

I was always broke.

Absurd, given that my salary and entrepreneurial income amounted to no small change. My salary and commission at ACM were a respectable seventy-five thousand a year. Add on another thirty-five grand gross, tax free-ish until the IRS caught up with me, selling prescription meds and weed, and I was bringing in one hundred-ten thousand annually, probably more.

Here's the rub. If I earned a hundred and ten thousand a year, I spent a hundred and twenty.

After I'd blown through my salary and cash on hand, I had a few other ways to generate cash—sell more drugs, ask friends for money, some plain old begging to people I hardly knew.

Mostly, I just hit up my mother.

I often texted, said, *I have to stay late again.*

You must love that job of yours. Your dad was the same way.

I do. I do, but, my boss is a douche bag.

Honey, you have to start somewhere, she said.

Tonight, I have to put together a presentation for Gabe. I'll email it to him late tonight. He'll present it to a client in the morning.

See you when you get home.

I texted, *Well, I, ah. I need like five hundred for a computer program. It sure would help with this presentation.*

I knew she didn't like me asking. I knew I created gobs of anxiety.

I did it anyway.

If you need it for work, she said. *I'll send it over now.*

Thank you.

159

Do you want me to save some dinner?

Another time, I called my mother, said I needed four thousand dollars to buy a Bloomberg Terminal, a computer system that enabled finance eggheads to monitor and analyze market data, place trades, and a bunch of other stuff. The fancier setups came with the computer and up to six screens. In my case, I told her I needed the software for my laptop.

I didn't need the Bloomberg Terminal, of course. We had one at the office I could use anytime. I needed the cash to buy drugs.

She said, "How do I know you'll spend the money on this, what's it called? A terminal?"

"Bloomberg Terminal. Market surveillance. Company research. Analytics. It's got it all."

"Matthew."

"Look," I said. "Once I buy the terminal, I'll send you a copy of my bank activity."

"It's a lot of money," my mother said.

"Full transparency. Really."

"A copy of your bank statement?"

"Once the sale goes through. Same day. I promise."

All true. What I didn't say was that I'd learned to jerry-rig my bank statements. Download a PDF version of my latest statement, open Adobe Acrobat, manipulate the PDF, amend the line item showing a four thousand dollar "branch withdrawal" to "Bloomberg Terminal," and voila. A master forger couldn't tell the difference.

The following day, I emailed the amended bank statement.

She texted, *I just saw the statement. Thank you for sending it, honey.*

Two months into my ACM tenure, I got a break. Gabe approached me, agitated, his normal state, said, "Tomorrow I want you to meet Kristin at Mr. Brooks' apartment. Kristin knows what to do. Go over his accounts, all the monthly review items."

"You want *me* there?" I asked.

"It's your account. Kristin is there for oversight."

"Me?"

"And Kristin. That's what I said."

Kristin was experienced, a few years older than me, a registered client associate qualified to initiate stock trades. She was nice, helpful, and willing to teach the new associates—everything Gabe wasn't.

Mr. Brooks' account had been arbitrarily assigned to me. Lately, he routinely called regarding wires, account information, and trades.

I was excited—a chance to meet with a client, at the client's apartment, no less, on the Upper East Side. I went home elated. I woke the next morning to a headache, puffy eyes, and then I peeked outside to see torrential rain. I wanted to crawl back in bed.

At Penn Station, I stumbled into a pizza place around eight-thirty a.m., ordered a coffee, and sipped. I had to be at Mr. Brooks' place in thirty minutes. I walked up the steps to the street level at Eighth Avenue, rain gushing down. I opened the Uber ride-sharing app on my phone. The wait time displayed ten minutes. No way I'd make it to the meeting on time.

I texted Kristin. *I just got off the train.*

Just?

It was delayed. I'm on my way now. I'll see you there.

K, she said.

I could tell she was furious. She knew I'd never make it in time. The Uber driver arrived, said it would take another fifteen minutes to reach the Upper East Side.

I rehearsed my excuse. Bad weather. Slow trains. Lackadaisical Uber drivers fresh from Syria or Somalia who didn't know the City. Gabe had all but ordered me to arrive fifteen minutes early, enough time to check into the lobby and proceed up to Mr. Brooks' penthouse apartment.

Kristin texted. *It's 9:02. Where are you?*

Almost there. Two minutes.

The driver dropped me at Fifty-Ninth and Park Avenue. I sprinted my way to the luxury apartment complex a few blocks away. I hadn't brought an umbrella.

I walked into the lobby drenched.

My hair was a mess.

Kristin glared at me, her frown showing pity and a good dose of anger.

We caught the elevator to the penthouse. The door opened to a gorgeous, windowpane apartment. Each wall of the apartment overlooking some unique angle of Manhattan I'd never seen. Bad weather and all, it was an amazing view.

I envisioned having this apartment. I'd sit next to a window, admiring the view, consuming all the pharma my body could process. I'd have all the money in the world to support my habit. Life would be easy. I'd no longer manipulate people. I'd give up my reckless ways. I wouldn't do stupid things. I was an associate with a dream.

In truth, I didn't want to work for it.

I wanted it handed to me.

Drugs had eroded my drive, my resolve, and replaced it with a fuzzy, withering euphoria that lasted only as long as I kept shoving dust up my nose.

What would my dad think of me? I know how he would have handled a similar meeting. He would have shown up fifteen minutes early, fully prepared, and on top of his game. He would have crushed the meeting.

I said, "We're late, Mr. Brooks. It's my fault. With the weather, I should have planned better."

Kristin rolled her eyes.

"I should have listened to Kristin here. She warned me."

Mr. Brooks said, "Matthew, it's about time we met in person."

"Please, Matt."

"Yes, well. You arrived safely. That's all that matters."

And like that, I pulled another rabbit out of a hat.

15

"LICENSE AND REGISTRATION, PLEASE."

I sat in my Rover, hot inside though it was cold outside. I looked up at the officer and said, "Here you go, sir."

I slipped my Policemen's Benevolent Association plastic card, often called a PBA card, under my license, and I handed it to the officer. The PBA card was given to me by a cop in town to help me get out of minor driving infractions. It was my get out of jail free card.

"I'll be right back," he said.

I said, "You never said why you stopped me."

"Fifty in a forty," he said. "Hang tight."

Remain calm, I told myself. *You're fine*. But was I? I felt my heart beating fast. Did I appear high? And if so, how high? I was good at keeping my cool. I'd gotten pulled over countless times, way too many, but I always got out of it. My engaging demeanor, no doubt. I watched him in the rearview mirror. Here he came, and I could tell by the way he walked back to my car I was in trouble.

It was November 2014. The air was brisk, wet with a coniferous smell—like it had flown in from Vermont.

"Sir, where did you say you're coming from?"

It was just shy of midnight on Tuesday. "The office," I said. "I work in New York City at ACM. I stayed late studying for my Series 7 exam."

"Ah, huh."

"My stockbroker's license."

"Is that right?"

This went on for a bit. I glanced at his badge, *Officer Bennett, Mendham Borough Police Department. New Jersey.* Then Officer Bennett circled round the back of my SUV to the passenger door.

What's this guy doing? I knew it was my own fault. I just had to smoke that fucking blunt before leaving Samson, my new supplier. Of all nights. And I forgot to douse myself in Febreze before I left—extra strength—to soak up some of the stink on me. I even forgot the eye drops. I was losing it.

Bennett walked behind my car, shouted at me. "Sir, please step out of the car."

"What did I do?" I shouted back.

When he reached the driver's window, he said, "The smell of marijuana, it's strong." He leaned over to look me in the eye. "It's coming from your car."

"That can't be."

"Do you have anything in your possession? Drugs of any kind?"

I opened my door and climbed down and shut the door behind me. "No, sir. I don't."

"Did you smoke weed tonight? Tell me the truth. I can get the K-9 unit here in ten minutes."

"I didn't," I said. "That's the truth." I looked at him. "Don't you need plausible cause, I mean, for a search?"

"You reek of weed. It's all the cause I need."

I put my hand on the door handle. "I am not letting you search my car."

"Do you have any drugs in the car?"

"I told you, I do not."

In fact, I did. Fifty oxycodone pills and 3 ounces of weed.

I was only two minutes from my destination, where I had planned to sell the weed, and then cruise on home to revel in my profits.

"Don't go anywhere," Bennett said.

An hour went by, me standing next to my Rover freezing my ass off before the K-9 unit arrived—another officer and a big hairy German shepherd. I could have waited for a warrant, I suppose, but I was high, tired, a little blurry, and I smelled of weed, so I knew a warrant was a foregone conclusion. I gave my consent. Search away. What's the worst that could happen? I get a few charges.

"If you could stand over there," the new officer pointed to a spot in front of my Rover, where I stood as the shepherd trotted up to my SUV, smelled weed, and took all of two seconds to find the source. Earlier, I was in that feebleminded state, not thinking at all, and I had put all my drugs in the driver's door compartment.

"Hands behind your back," Officer Bennett said.

I spun around, put my arms behind my back—the rough breeze blew against my face as I looked up.

He placed the handcuffs on my wrists. They were cold and heavy, unlike the toy replica I had as a kid.

This was really happening.

I got to the station and was re-handcuffed to a chair in the holding area.

Another officer, a big guy with no hair, asked me to cooperate. All I had to do was rat on my dealers. No way. I thought of myself as a kind of outlaw, not a wise guy exactly, but a guy who kept his mouth shut. Coming from a strictly Italian family, I knew better than to rat. Besides, ratting wouldn't get me anywhere. The cop said otherwise, but I knew the truth.

Officer Bennett uncuffed me, walked me to a scuffed metal table in the center of the room, and re-cuffed me to a chair beside the desk. He sat and looked at the paperwork in front of him, said, "Looks like two felony charges to me. Plus, one more—intent to distribute. You understand what kind of trouble you're in? Operating a vehicle with illegal narcotics? It's more serious than you think."

Two cops from Randolph, New Jersey, a little town north of there, came into the station, looked over at me and laughed. One of the officers walked my way, said, "Where are you coming from, all dressed up?"

I sat there in my wrinkled Ralph Lauren suit, subtle gray stripe, wool, classic fit, notch lapel, flat-front slacks.

"I work in Midtown," I said.

"I'm sure you do."

"Archibald Capital Management, as I told Officer Bennett here, studying for my Series 7."

"What's that?"

"General securities exam."

"You peddle stocks?"

"Once I pass my Series 7, I will."

He shook his head, turned away. "We snared a stockbroker."

I was a mess, my tie hanging limp, my Esquire-blue shirt wrinkled. I was sweating. From a distance, I could be a budding stockbroker or an overeager drug dealer trying to impress.

"Come with me," Bennett said.

I got up and took some mug shots. Great. People said I had my dad's nose. I would forever be memorialized by a mug shot.

I sat in the station for another three hours. I didn't rat. I waited for a lawyer.

Whenever there were two or more officers in the room, they glanced at me and laughed.

The other officers were morons. Bennett, him I was on the fence about. I still believed I could get one past him. Initially, I told Bennett the pills were Adderall, a prescription for which I legally had. I said I'd bring the bottle tomorrow. He looked at each pill, four different sizes and shapes, plugged the pill imprints into an online application, and voila, the pills in the bottle were not Adderall at all.

Bennett didn't even look up. "What we found in your SUV, turns out is oxycodone."

"I don't know what to say. Try it again."

"This isn't my first arrest, kid. Look, I got some paperwork to do. Sit tight."

It took another hour and a half to print my arrest summons. Bennett might have been top-notch when it came to issuing speeding tickets and trapping Midtown traders on a bender, but he was worthless on a computer. The station paperwork was stored in a PDF format, and he and the other numbnuts couldn't figure out that each new PDF form opened in a new tab. *Gee, where'd everything go?*

When I caught him alone, I tried to persuade Bennett to give me some pills. "Come on, man," I begged. "It won't matter. Just ten pills. What's the difference? You're charging me with a felony. So do it with ten less pills."

Bennett stared at me. "You're a piece of work."

Well then, go fuck yourself, I thought to myself.

I wanted to punch him in the head, take the pills, and run.

I felt the anxiety creeping up on me. Some mischievous withdrawal symptoms were just around the corner.

Bennett said, "You lied to me. Understandable. Other than that, you've been polite. That counts for something. You can go."

"The pills?" I asked.

"Take your paperwork and get out of here."

I left with three court summons detailing my arrest and charges, and an upcoming court date to plead guilty or not guilty.

When I got home, I searched my room for a little blue oxy I might have dropped—under the bed, behind the desk, just one, or a half, or a little pile of opioid alkaloid dust I might have overlooked. One puny pill.

I didn't find anything.

I had some Suboxone in my desk. Didn't want to take it. It might ease the pain of withdrawal, but I could do better. If I took the Suboxone, I couldn't get high for a day or longer, assuming I found an errant oxycodone pill. The mix would mess with me bad. I'd rather suffer withdrawal.

I lay in my bed watching *Family Guy*. Then my body went berserk, legs restless and achy. A few moments later, I got the leg shakes, the muscles of my thighs jerking me around. I was possessed. Then the shaking spread to my chest and arms and head.

I just remembered I had some Xanax stashed away in a drawer. I made it to the desk, yanked on the drawer, and dumped the whole drawer out on the carpet. Found three bars, and swallowed two.

I needed to ingest oxycodone soon or it wouldn't be good. My skin felt like spiders were crawling all over—neck, face, up my nose—it was awful. I couldn't maintain my emotions, I started crying and, suddenly, laughing, and then some in between weepy state.

Then the Xanax kicked in, and I passed out.

The day before, on my way out of the office, Gabe reminded me to show up at ACM's Jericho office on the North Shore of Long Island the following day. Gabe regularly worked out of the Long Island office because it was ten minutes from his house. Occasionally, he'd have me join him—I think so he could keep an eye on me.

I hadn't fallen asleep until five a.m.

Gabe called around eight and left a voicemail message. "Where the fuck are you?"

Without pills, no way I could make it work. Sure, I was risking my job. Didn't matter. I didn't have the strength to roll over. Zero strength to call back and supplicate myself to my boss.

I waited for him to call again, which he did. "You're late," he screamed at me.

"Gabe. I'm sick. I'm sorry, but no way I can make it today."

"Too sick to pick up a phone?"

"Uh-huh."

"You really fucked me," he said. "You know that? You have the documents I need."

I was nauseous. I held back a gag. "Right, right."

"Look. I'll have Karuna send a UPS pickup."

"UPS?"

"To your house."

"I don't feel well."

"Give whoever it is the documents. Is that too much to ask?"

I barfed in the trashcan next to my bed.

Gabe said, "What the fuck was that?"

Nothing but bile, I wanted to say.

I heard my mother's voice before I understood the words. I'd fallen asleep, was still drowsy. "Matthew," she shouted.

"Mom, please," I shouted through my closed door.

"The UPS guy is out front. Get down here."

"Come up," I half-shouted, all the energy draining from my body. "Please." This last word was no more than a whisper.

She climbed the stairs, banged on my locked door.

I barely had the strength to get up and open the door.

"Here, give him these." I handed over a bunch of papers.

She was shocked at the sight of me. "Honey, what's wrong with you?"

"I'm sick. Food poisoning, I think. Go give him the papers. Gabe's waiting."

I spent the next two days in bed.

Called in sick Thursday and Friday.

I tried to arrange a time for Samson to come to my house, but I dozed off every twenty minutes and missed his return calls. I didn't have the oomph to leave. Even if I did, my mother would know something was up.

I called my uncle Tony, the lawyer, a litigator no less, and fessed up to the whole mess.

The first thing he said was, "Tell your mother."

"You think that's a good idea?"

"I do. Tell her now. Give me a few minutes, and I'll conference you with a colleague, a criminal lawyer. When I call back, answer the fucking phone."

"I will. I promise."

Tony called back a little later, introduced me to another attorney, the guy's name I forgot the instant I heard it. My head wasn't working right.

"Before we get started," Tony said. "The arrest was for weed. That's the issue here. No alcohol."

While I fessed up about the weed, I didn't mention the pills. I said, "No alcohol. I promise."

"Good, okay then."

I almost couldn't get the words out. "And some pills."

Tony was angry. I could hear it in the silence. "How many and what?"

"Fifty. Oxycodone."

"What the fuck?" Tony shouted. "You didn't say anything about illegal prescription painkillers!"

The animosity in his voice was so abrupt it took me by surprise. I started to cry. "I know. I'm sorry."

"What are you doing with that many pills?"

"Nothing, really."

"Are you selling them?" And when I didn't answer, he said, "It doesn't matter. We'll figure this out. Sit tight. I'll make some more calls. Talk to your mom in the meantime."

"I will."

I don't think the other guy said a word.

16

BEFORE I COULD CONFESS TO my mother, I thought it best to get Samson over to the house with some blues. No way I could talk to my mother, and Joe, in the middle of a meltdown. One conversation at a time. Addiction and withdrawal first. Arrest second.

I called Samson. "I really need you to head this way. I need blues, bad."

"I don't make house calls."

"I'll pay. For the drive over. Your time, gas, everything."

"I could make an exception."

"The thing is," I said. "I don't have any cash. Not this moment. We'll square up tomorrow, I swear."

"Something about this deal doesn't sound right."

"I'm hurting bad. I'm asking for a favor. Please. I'm on the verge of going crazy here."

"Dude, you always fucking say that."

Samson was thirtyish, bald, a short rock, did a lot of ste-roids and weight lifting in his past. Not a guy to mess with, but a softy if he liked you. "All right," he said. "Give me like forty minutes."

"You've no idea how much this helps."

"Hey, and don't call me anytime soon. I'll be there when I get there."

Forty minutes to a dealer was sort of flextime. It meant any-thing he wanted it to mean.

Christmas was coming early. I grinned from ear to ear. Once my order arrived, the opiate would promptly make everything better. Until then, I flipped on the television in my room, and I found an episode of *Family Guy* I hadn't seen.

Eventually, Samson called and said he was in my driveway.

I texted back. *Meet you at the barn, around the corner of the house.*

It was cold outside—black ice was scattered amongst the stones in the rocky path connected to the driveway. I stumbled out the front door barefoot and did my best to maneuver around it. I was weak and couldn't even think about putting shoes on. My body was on autopilot. I slowly stumbled to the barn. Sam-son was still in his car, and I waved him inside.

He handed me ten pills. They were As, my favorite. The 30-milligram version was blue with the code "A 215" carved on one side, a narcotic analgesic used for chronic pain, but for me, it was my fix. I picked up a plastic card I had on a shelf and a bill to break down the pills. I grabbed four pills, placed each on a little white table in the corner, laid the bill over the pills and then the card and pressed hard. Nothing. I was too weak to crush a few pills.

I looked at Samson who stared at me. "Can you break these down for me?"

He looked at me with such disdain. As if he pitied me. I was a nuisance to him, but he also wanted to help and knew I was sick. I didn't care how weak I looked to him—I needed to feel normal again.

"Bro. Get out of the way."

The moment the powder went up my nose, I got a chill, more of a shake or a tremor. A super-fast twitch.

And just like that, I was on my way to feeling better again, this warm sensation pulsating throughout my body. All I could do was sit back and taste the drip down the back of my throat. I was in a peaceful place; all my problems were gone.

I snorted what remained of the powdered blue, thanked Samson, and told him I would call him the next day. Shit, I gave him a hug. He charged me double, maybe triple. Oh, well. All I cared about was the high.

I snuck back inside the house, ran up to my room to snort another couple of pills.

That's when I decided to give the news to my mother.

I found her in the kitchen.

A blank, sunken-in look on my face, she said. "What's wrong? What happened?"

"Sit down," I said and waved my hand at one of the bar stools.

"I don't like the sound of this."

No evasion. No waffling. I said, "I got arrested the other night. Tuesday...no, Wednesday."

"Arrested? For what?" her face flashing from one of curiosity to anger—maybe disappointment.

She seemed to sink into the oversized sweatshirt she was wearing. My dad's, I think. It was as if my words completely crushed her little heart.

"Possession of narcotics."

"Come with me." She ushered me into my dad's office, away from any big ears in the house. Shouted for Joe to join us.

In the office, I stared at the photos on the wall, several of my father. My father had short, dark brown hair, perfectly quaffed back, whereas I had jet black hair like my mom. He had an Italian-looking nose, like me, long with a slight curve in the middle. I was a hybrid of my parents—I got my looks mostly from my mom but personality strictly from my dad. My work ethic? Mine alone.

"Now," she said, "Tell us what this is about."

I looked at Joe. "I was pulled over for speeding, and the officer found oxycodone and weed in my car."

"Yours?" my mother asked. "These were your pills? You're doing the pills again?"

"No. I was selling them to a friend. A way to make a few extra dollars, that's all."

Joe said, "You're not doing drugs?"

"No."

My mother reached up and touched my hand. "Matthew?"

I said, "I swear I am not doing pills. Not again."

"Go on," Joe said.

"I called Uncle Tony. He set up a meeting with a lawyer for tomorrow morning."

Why couldn't I just come clean, you ask? Because I didn't have the guts to tell my mom I fucked up. I was embarrassed. And worst of all, my dad was staring down at all of us. I especially couldn't fess up in front of him.

My mom and I pulled up to the lawyer's office in Roseland, New Jersey. Uncle Tony's BMW was already in the parking lot.

"Mom, we really gotta talk about paying this dealer back."

"Yes, I know Matthew, one thing at a time please," she remarked. I could hear the anger in her voice. She was pissed, and I knew that by her Brooklyn accent coming out more with each word fully pronounced.

We walked inside. I made a quick run to the bathroom to crush and snort a blue. We were invited into the lawyer's office and sat down. We introduced ourselves. The lawyer's name was Ralph M. Ricci. Attorneys loved their middle initials. He said he focused on criminal and civil trial litigation. A few DWI defense cases. As a litigator, he had handled a number of high profile criminal matters, a few notable police and other public employee disciplinary matters, though what this had to do with me wasn't clear.

When it was my turn, I told him about the arrest.

Ricci said, "I see this as a relapse. The drugs were for your personal use."

Tony nodded.

"My son," my mother said, "Matthew, here, says the drugs were for someone else."

"How can I say this?" Ricci said. "That story will get you in a whole lot of trouble, assuming we could prove it true."

I stared at the carpet, a kind of rust-colored Berber, I think, said, "They *were* for my personal use."

My mother glanced at me, unsure if I was confessing some new shame, or just going along with the plan to save my ass.

Ricci said, "Right. I'll do my best to get you conditional discharge. Pretrial intervention, PTI, at worst."

Tony said, "Tell us about pretrial intervention."

"You get PTI once. This is it. In which case, you meet with a probation officer from time to time. Conditional discharge would be better, but with the quantity of drugs you had in your possession, it'll be hard to pull off." Ricci looked competent, mustache and goatee against his dark face, the goatee going white. He thought for a moment, said, "I'm going to work hard for conditional discharge."

"Conditional discharge," my mother repeated, just to hear the sound of it.

Ricci said, "In the meantime, you get into treatment as soon as possible. Today, if you can."

"What kind of treatment?" my mother asked.

"It doesn't have to be rehab. I'd go with an intensive outpatient program. I will contact the Mendham Police Department and get a copy of the arrest tape."

Ricci looked at me.

I said, "IOP. I'll look into it today." I was still so hellbent on staying high, that I wouldn't let it happen—and turns out, it didn't.

My mom took out her checkbook, wrote him a check for $5,000, something she must have discussed with Tony in advance.

I walked out, confident the felony charges would be dropped. Ricci was on top of his game, or so it seemed. Outside, the sun beamed down on my face, a late-fall morning, and a good one at that.

One hiccup. I needed more pills. I felt a hint of withdrawal creeping up on me.

Not yet to the car, I said, "About what we talked about earlier—"

My mother was not happy with me. Her arms crossed, her eyes beaming through mine. "I didn't forget," she said. "This dealer of yours, he has to have his money today?"

"Or I'm in trouble. I gave him my word."

"Your word," she said, and I expected to hear more, but it didn't come.

"You'll transfer the money?"

"Five thousand? On top of the money I just paid Mr. Ricci to get you out of this mess?"

"I know it's a lot to ask," I said.

"And once you pay this guy, what's his name again?"

"I didn't say. Best you don't know."

"Well, once you pay this guy, you part ways with him. Are we clear?"

"I know. I know. I mean, yes, we're clear."

In truth, I owed Samson around three thousand. I pocketed the rest, just enough to get a couple hundred pills for the long weekend ahead.

That afternoon, there I was driving to Newark to pick up more pills, my body and mind on autopilot. No matter how much I wanted to turn the car around, I just kept driving. I felt guilty. I really did. But even with the guilt accumulating with each mile, I just kept driving.

I got a text from my mother. *Please get help.*

I will, I promise, I texted back.

I don't want to bury you. We've been through enough.

I did want to get help. I just didn't want to stop taking drugs.

Somewhere along the line, I came to realize that I would never figure out the details of my dad's story. What I did know was that the people trapped in his office, him included, had to fight to breathe in clear oxygen and were so desperate to survive. For me, my survival instincts had to do with whether or not I could get more drugs. That's all I cared about, and that's what I needed in order to continue living, even though drugs were slowly killing me day by day. There must have been some indescribable conditions to cause people to jump, or to even think it was the best way to die. In that brief moment, they must have felt free, alive. I was dying to find my own sense of freedom, and it felt as if I could never find the courage or strength to get to the other side of it. I felt that I was always going to be trapped in this life.

17

THE TAIL END OF 2014 concluded an eventful year. I walked into a Wells Fargo Bank branch in NYC and withdrew a thousand dollars, well over my ATM limit. If I had a big score in the works, I wanted extra cash on hand, just because. Still, I couldn't help but wonder—what if I got robbed? It could happen. What if some asshole sold me fake pills? Either way, I'd have cash in my pocket to resupply.

After leaving the bank, I got on the train at Penn Station, made a quick stop in Newark for a buy. Dre picked me up at Broad Street Station. I hopped in his Dodge Challenger, and we drove around the block while he doled out thirty of my favorite blues, A-215s. I had plenty of Xanax and weed at home, so I just needed enough oxy to last the night and next day.

Dre pulled over and twisted away from me, looking out the window behind him. Poking out of his pocket, I saw a slim black pistol, a Glock 42, .380 auto, 5.94 inches, long muzzle to back strap. According to Dre, at least. He was proud of his gun and had shown it off a couple of weeks ago. The smallest on the market, he said.

"I'll see you tomorrow," I said, got out, and walked back to Broad Street Station. I had such a feeling of relief every time I scored, semi-dazed thinking about my precious pills. And my good feeling affected my mood in general. For the first time that day, I noticed the early winter evening surrounding me, the old brick clock tower in front of me. I smiled from ear to ear, the air crisp and cool, me in my expensive suit and salmon-colored tie flapping in the wind.

I jogged up the train station corridor toward the bathroom.

I didn't need to consume. I just wanted to count the pills, touch them.

The bathroom stunk of homeless people. I found a stall, closed and locked the door, and pulled out a stock analyst report on BP P.L.C. (formerly British Petroleum), my temporary platform. I pulled the baggie of blues from my pocket and opened it, started counting. Two, four, six.

I heard two voices, loud and clear. Cops. I stuffed the open baggie in my suit pocket.

"Hey, you," the voice coming from above me said.

I looked up and saw two ugly faces, police officers peeking over the old wooden stall door.

One of the officers said, "Get out here."

"I'm not doing anything wrong," I said.

"Sir, I'm asking you to come out of the stall. Now."

I opened the stall door and moved tentatively forward. Two cops, one short, the other normal, average, nondescript.

The short one said, "Empty your fucking pockets."

I sort of threw my arms in the air. You mean me? I said, "I'm not even doing anything. You definitely can't hover over the door like that."

The short cop marched a step closer and pointed at my jacket pocket. I pulled the pills from my pocket.

"Where did you get these?"

"My grandmother," I said. "They're hers. I took them from her bottle today. She knows I have them."

The key to dealing with cops, be polite.

The normal cop said, "Let me see your license, please."

I pulled out my wallet, handed him my driver's license, said, "I can call my grandma if you'd like."

"This would help how?"

"She knows I have the pills. I have a bad back."

"That won't be necessary," he said. He handed back my license.

"Thank you. I can't tell you how much I appreciate your understand—"

The short officer handed me the baggie of pills, said, "Flush them."

Wait what? These two were making me flush my fucking pills? This had to be some sort of joke. The short guy glared at me. I turned, faced the open toilet bowl. I stood there for a long time, then slowly dropped one pill at a time into the mold-infested toilet, each pill worth around twenty dollars. I counted in my head, twenty, forty, sixty...

I dropped a few pills on the ground, hoping they wouldn't notice.

"Kid, are you serious?"

"I'm nervous," I said.

The normal officer said, "We're doing you a favor. Pick those up and flush them."

The short officer said, "Be quick about it."

I just put six hundred dollars in the toilet.

The short cop was enjoying himself. He laughed at his buddy, then pointed at me. "Flush it."

"I can't."

The normal cop was tired of the whole thing, agitated, not smiling, in a hurry to move on, or just get out of this stinking bathroom. He said, "Flush the fucking toilet or you're coming with us."

So I pushed on the little fake-chrome handle.

He said, "You don't have anything else on you, right?"

"No, sir, I do not," I said.

"No heroin?"

"Shit no. Why would I have that?"

"You walked in about the time our favorite shitbag heroin dealer walked out. You sure you don't have anything else on you?"

"No, sir. I mean—yes, sir, I do not."

"Get the hell out of here."

Rather than count my blessings, hop on the train home and call it a night, I wandered the station waiting area, thinking, staring at the polished floors and tall ceilings and dark wood trim on the windows and doors. I pulled my phone and tapped the Wells Fargo app, looked for the closest ATM machine. Found one west of the station, hopped in a cab, gave the cabbie directions.

I called Dre. "I need you to come grab me again."

"You got to slow down."

"Some bullshit with the pigs. All good, though. My problem, not yours. Another thirty Bs. I'm heading to the ATM now."

"All right, Matty. Be there in a little."

I was politely asked to leave ACM in February. I failed the Series 7, so one of the mutants in HR gave me a month to find a new position.

I said, "I was nine lousy points short."

"I'm sure you'll do better next time," the HR lady said.

In my defense, I wanted to say I would have passed if I weren't so high. Closer to blitzed. I snorted six blues just before the test. Another four at the break. The last four might have been a bad idea.

In March, I accepted a temporary position at Credit Principale, a French equity broker that provided institutional investors with equity research, a focus on Pan-European equity markets. For the longest time, I gave myself so much credit that I was able to land these jobs on Wall Street as a full-blown addict. If these companies would hire me, maybe I wasn't that bad after all?

For a bit over two months on the job, I hung in there. I performed research for the firm's European equity department. Not days after I started, I made a commitment to myself to show up early, leave late. I would reincarnate myself as my dad and do what he did, day after day, until he worked his way up. Wake up at five, out the door by six, and get home at eight.

Fat chance.

Each morning at seven a.m., a small team of New York traders and analysts had a video chat with a similar team in the Paris office. The teams talked stocks and news and latest earnings, how they might pitch one stock or another to clients. I was asked to sit in. Learn something. *I'd love to.*

Over the next month and a half, I made two lousy video conferences.

In April 2015, I finally got word on the drug arrest: a year of probation. My attorney, Ricci, finagled the conditional discharge.

I was lucky.

I had some time before my first random drug test, so my pharma intake didn't change much, if at all.

In May, I met up with a fraternity brother, Tyler Myers, a couple years older than me. We had dinner, got high, and talked about old times. The next day, I texted, asked to meet for coffee.

Tyler texted back. *Heading home to NJ. On the train now. Another time.*

The following day I got a call from one of my friends who graduated with Tyler. Apparently Tyler had gotten fired the day I suggested coffee, then picked up a bunch of drugs and overdosed. He was twenty-six years old.

I felt guilty. Would things have turned out different if we met for coffee?

I attended Tyler's wake high, feigning sobriety. Did a half-ass job of it.

Two weeks later, another overdose—an acquaintance from Villanova.

I had a lot of shit rumbling around in my head. I was addicted, no question. I couldn't quit, no question there either. I had random drug tests to look forward to. The pesky issue of probation and a hardnosed probation officer grilling me on a regular basis. Now a couple of people I knew, real human beings with real lives, up and died for no convincing reason. Life was bleak.

Here's a question that occasionally floated to the top. *What if I ended it?* My life.

It was a good fucking question.

The upside with this thinking was I could just end it all, no more withdrawals, no more scheming for money, no more lying, and I wouldn't be a burden on everyone who loved me anymore. They would be better off without me. The downside—put my family through another tragedy, leave my mother heartbroken and lost, my brothers without an emotionally, nonexistent brother. Would the escape be worth it, or would I be a coward for doing it? My father didn't jump.

I didn't have a good answer.

One day I worked late, finished whatever was assigned to me, and then started surfing the internet. I don't know what I was looking for, back to the same 9/11 shit, but I came across the story of Madison Holleran, a UPenn student who killed herself by jumping off the roof of a parking garage in Philadelphia. She was pretty and young, a collegiate athlete. She suffered from depression. Add on the pressures of attending a prestigious university, and she was toast. The story, the girl, it all fascinated me.

What went through her mind before she jumped? Did she find the freedom she had been searching for in the few seconds of free fall?

I glanced across the work floor at the conference room, at the long table and leather chairs and those floor to ceiling windows. I thought of the view from the twenty-sixth floor, how the buses looked like little toy cars, the cheap ones made in China. I thought about how this wasn't a quarter of the height of the World Trade Center towers, and if I jumped out the window, I would surely die. I thought about taking the elevator to the roof, another twenty stories up, walking to the edge of the building, pausing, then jumping.

I turned off my computer, tidied up my desk, then took the elevator down, not up. I walked all the way to the Upper East Side, a good forty-minute hike. On the way, I called my grandma and talked to her about this cute, athletic girl, Madison Holleran, I'd read about.

She said, "You need to stop reading that stuff."

"She had everything going for her."

"It's morbid," she said. "It doesn't do you any good."

"I know," I said, and I did. Maybe I was attracted to morbid. I said, "Even when it looks like you have it all, you might have nothing."

"I don't like this kind of talk."

"I don't like thinking it."

My mind worked okay most of the time, aside from the constant dark thoughts and mental flatness—drugs no longer provided the defibrillating shock I was used to. My body was falling apart—the drugs, the excess weight, a waterworks of sweat I couldn't shut off. I felt my body and mind and whatever else there was to me were all separate entities. Half the time, they fought with each other. And me, the thing that was me, was cocooned inside this sweaty, depressed shell.

As I sat reading Madison Holleran's story, I had the strangest thought. Madison wasn't fine for some time before she jumped. I wasn't fine, I knew it, and maybe it was obvious to those around me. Maybe my 9/11 nightmares would come true and I could do exactly what Madison did and just leap and end it all. Maybe I could be free.

But I didn't want to be a jumper.

I should ask for help.

At the same time, I hated admitting defeat. I hated asking anyone for anything. I grew up doing things for myself—homework, projects, getting ready for school. Small things, perhaps, but I did them without help. And later on, I got myself into college, created a little drug selling empire for myself.

I should ask for help. I should.

A friend from Villanova, Kirby, was apartment sitting for his older brother. He invited me to spend the night, kick it, maybe get high. I was broke, so I asked him to spot me some cash. A thousand dollars, eleven hundred would be better. I'd cop us some blues. Ten minutes later, I had the money in my Chase account.

Kirby was a good guy, but I still charged him more than I paid. Friend or no friend, I had a habit to support.

I took the elevator to the twentieth floor, knocked on the door. Kirby answered all smiles. The place was in the Upper East Side overlooking Manhattan, big windows, brown leather couches facing a giant flat-screen TV. It was time to get high. I had fifty blues between us. Plus, an ounce of weed in my overnight bag. Kirby had xannies.

Snort blues, swallow xannies, inhale weed. Repeat.

An hour later, we ordered sushi. I ate four California rolls all by myself and fell back on the cushy couch to enjoy my high.

"Nice place," I said.

"Did you see the safe?"

"What, where?"

"In his bedroom. My brother's a nut for security. Or maybe he just doesn't trust me with his shit."

"What's inside?"

"Don't know. Let's figure it out."

"Sounds like a plan, B." Our little thing. We called each other B, short for Bro.

We walked into his brother's bedroom, a massive space, a monochrome of browns and blues. The safe was waist-high behind a dark wood cabinet door. The front of the safe was polished gray with a black keypad in the center.

"What's the combination?" I asked.

Kirby rolled his eyes. He punched in some numbers. Nothing.

Tried again. Still nothing.

"Think, dude," I said. "Really think. Birthdate, phone number, part of a social, maybe."

"I'm thinking. I'm thinking."

Kirby pressed more numbers. Bingo. A tiny light on the face of the keypad lit up.

"Open it," Kirby said.

"You think we should?"

"We've come this far."

Inside was a bunch of pill bottles, nearly all of them Xanax or a generic. I read the closest bottle, 2 milligram green bars called Hulks, and next to it a bottle of 2 milligram yellow bars referred to as School Buses, and next to that a half-full bottle of 1 milligram oval blue pills called Footballs. Several more pill bottles. Shit, I was in heaven.

I looked at Kirby. We were both grinning, our heads almost touching, his pupils big as dimes. I said, "What now?"

"We take a few each from each bottle."

"Sounds good," I said.

Before the night was over, we'd take way more than a few. I knew it, and Kirby knew it.

In the morning, I called my mother. "I need eighteen hundred dollars to give to Kirby. I know. I know. Before you yell at me, it was all my fault."

"What now?" she shouted into the phone.

"We were drunk. I broke one of his brother's antique vases." Not true, but his brother was a collector, and the story was plausible.

"Every day it's something different with you."

"Mom, please. We found a place in the City. If I pay soon, they can deliver it before his brother gets home."

"What's the name of the place?"

"It's in the City," I said. "I forget the exact name."

"But it has a name, am I right?"

"Let me look here. Here it is. Syl-Lee Antiques. With a hyphen in the middle."

"This place, Syl-Lee with the hyphen, they just happen to have the exact same vase?"

"A different one, but Kirby says the gesture may smooth things over."

"Eighteen hundred dollars." Her voice was thick with sarcasm, a tone she rarely used. "It must be stunning."

"I don't know. Some pale green and yellows. A bunch of flowers around the neck. Nippon stamped on the base, Kirby says it means it's rare."

"You broke a rare Asian vase?"

"Japanese, I think. All my fault. I've got to make it right. I'll send you a photo of the new vase. Not new, an old one, a replacement. About the same size."

"I can't deal with this right now," she said and abruptly hung up the phone.

I found a ridiculously priced Nippon vase on eBay, almost four thousand dollars. I pay half. Kirby pays half. Sounded reasonable. I owed Kirby a few hundred for the drugs. The rest would cover my score for the day.

I sent my mother a photo of the vase.

She texted, *This is the last time, Matthew.*

Never again. I promise.

Credit Principale's New York offices were located in Midtown. The daily commute back to New Vernon was wearing thin, so I took to crashing on my buddy Jake's couch on the Upper East Side.

Jake was far from a stellar influence. Each night after work, we smoked a few joints of Lemon Haze. In the morning, before Jake or his roommate Gus woke, I snorted a couple of blues, maybe a line of coke. If I woke at five like I was supposed to, I had plenty of time to self-medicate, grab a caramel Frappuccino at Starbucks, and relax in the cab ride to the office. More often than not, however, I slept through my alarm and woke when Gus got up at nine a.m.

I sent the HR lady another bullshit-ridden email. My tardiness was so habitual, she stopped responding to my excuses. I think she knew after my probationary period ended that I would not be invited to stick around, so I didn't even bother.

One bright spring day in the conference room, twenty-six floors up, admiring the view—the Empire State Building and behind it in the distance, the Freedom Tower. I thought of 9/11. Couldn't help it.

I sat in one of the black leather chairs, waiting for Ree, a new dealer, to call back. I'd ordered twenty oxy and twenty xannie bars. I kicked back and crossed my fat legs. I had gained so much weight over the past couple of years my entire body had swollen. People told me I was letting myself go. Each time I heard it, I got defensive and then did nothing about it. I looked down at Fifth Avenue, watched the city buses driving this way and that, reading the numbers painted on the roof—3461, 4823—and wondered how many buses were out in the City this very minute. I thought about my dad on 9/11, how he went to work just like any normal day, and how no one would imagine the inconceivable notion that planes would be flown into office buildings. I imagined my dad, strong and courageous, trying to find a way out of the burning building while people all around him decided jumping to their deaths would be the quickest way to confront an inevitable death. Those thoughts disappeared as quickly as they came into my mind, especially because I was starting to feel withdrawal symptoms creep up and knew that my strenuous habit would need to be fulfilled as soon as possible.

I was also nervous. I needed cash, and I needed it quick. I wasn't worried so much about a deal not coming through as I was not having the money to pay for the deal I'd set up.

I'd come up with a new scheme to get money. Here it was: Create a dummy PayPal account with an innocuous business name—say VV Discount (a cheesy derivation on my favorite tie-maker Vineyard Vines)—send money from one of my mother's credit cards to the VV Discount account, then transfer the money from the VV Discount account to my personal PayPal account, and finally withdraw the cash at an ATM and buy drugs.

I hit some kind of PayPal transfer limit, some bullshit fraud or security trigger. There had to be a workaround.

I called Kirby, who lived in the Upper East Side. He had a PayPal account. He ignored my call, so I texted. *Kirby call me ASAP. It's important.*

He texted, *I'm in the middle of a haircut.*

I need a favor. I'm going to send you money via PayPal. I need you to send it back to my personal account. I'm picking up later. I'll throw you a bone for your help.

I got you. Can I add five to the order?

Let me call my guy, I said. *Send the money in the meantime.*

Then I called Ree in Newark, who didn't answer and didn't get back to me.

I couldn't wait. I'd buy from my Midtown delivery guys. The price was double, sometimes more, but I was in a hurry. In Newark, I paid sixteen dollars a pill if I bought in bulk, twenty dollars a pill for onesies and twosies. My Midtown guys charged a flat thirty-five dollars per pill, minimum of four pills. No discount for bulk purchases, a lousy business model, from my perspective.

I texted Kirby and told him about the change in plans and price.

No problem. I'm at John Allen's on 46th and Lex. Meet at Chase on the corner and I'll give you my cash?

John Allen's was the trendy barbershop in the City. Cuts ran a hundred bucks or some such nonsense.

I texted Young, one of my Midtown delivery service contacts, and he responded quicker than normal, telling me he'd be at Forty-Seventh and Park Avenue, a long block west of Lexington Avenue, in ten minutes.

I ran out of the office at Credit Principale on Fifth, sort of jogged east to meet Kirby on Lexington Avenue.

My cell vibrated. Young. "Where you at?"

The one time I needed extra time, Young was on point.

I met Kirby, grabbed the money, then bolted back the same way I'd just come to meet Young. Spotted his black Audi A4 on the corner of Park Ave and I climbed in.

"What's up, bro?" Young was black with a thin line for a mustache and buzz cut on top.

"Same old shit," I said. He drove a few blocks, we did the swap, and he gave me the go-ahead to hop out.

Young said, "You're good. Don't be a stranger."

Fifteen minutes later, I gave Kirby his pills. A lot of work for one buy.

I walked back to the office, took the elevator to the twenty-sixth floor, and opened the double glass doors—*Credit Principale* carved across the glass. I walked straight to my desk. The best part about being the last serf in the office was that I didn't have to sneak to the bathroom to do my drugs. I grabbed a stock report one of the Paris office analysts had written about Louis Vuitton and walked to the conference room. I sat and crushed six oxys atop the report. I separated the lines into two thin lines, which would make it easier to snort. The blue lines were skinny enough, and I looked at them and thought of the Twin Towers. I rolled a bill and snorted the baby-blue powder, leaned back, stretched, and stared at the ceiling. With my feet on the desk, I waited for my high to kick in.

One of the cleaning ladies, a Russian with a heavy accent, came into the conference room, saw me looking up. She asked, "Are you okay, sir?"

"Working late," I said. I tapped the report in front of me, the residue of blue powder on the front page, proof of my guileless work ethic. "I'm fine. Thank you for asking."

18

UNCLE PHIL CAME INTO MY room late one night when I was fifteen. We were down the beach for the week with his family, and I had all but avoided him the best I could. This night I could not. I could smell whiskey on his breath. My body froze as he took his big, swollen hands and forced them on top of mine. He got on top of me and began sodomizing me, covering my mouth shut with his right hand so no one could hear my screams.

"You have an ass like a little girl," he said.

I was bleeding everywhere and felt like a beaten-up rag doll.

Then I frantically woke up. My hands sweaty, my face clammy. I turned to my left and looked at myself in the mirror of the guest room of my grandma's house. A picture of Phil, my aunt, and cousins was on the dresser.

I started having these nightmares about Phil randomly that summer, probably because of the fear of him being right down the street from me. But now, I was having nightmares about things that didn't even happen, and I had no idea where these thoughts were coming from. The proximity to Phil was starting to mess with my head.

Sometime in June 2015, my mother and Joe and my brothers trooped off for the summer to stay in our beach house on Long Beach Island. For a couple of months, I stayed at my grandma Laura's house in Florham Park, New Jersey. I had loved sleeping over my grandma's house as a kid. I still loved it as a teenager and twenty-something because she treated me like a king. She let me stay up late watching TV, and then made a big breakfast in the morning. The summer of 2015 felt like one long sleepover.

I was twenty-three and, in some ways, still a kid. My mother preferred I stay at my grandma's house rather than stay alone. Likely, she suspected I was still getting high but didn't say anything, at least not to me. Perhaps, she didn't want me to do something stupid, like overdose with no one in the house to dial 911. Not long ago, she'd banged on my door, and when that didn't rouse me, she broke in and found me conscious but incoherent.

Grandma had one niggling rule: I had to be home and inside the house every night by eight. And she didn't go to bed early like my mom, so if I was late, she'd know.

The thrill of living with my grandmother, notwithstanding, I grew more and more depressed as the summer wore on.

I remember the day I confessed: July 8, 2015. And by confessed, I mean wrote a suicide note on my phone.

I woke, hopped in the shower, and then got dressed. I walked into the bathroom to snort a couple of blues before heading to the train station. I glanced in the mirror and didn't recognize myself. On the outside, I looked okay—crisp navy suit, lavender tie, pressed white French-cuff shirt, and a pair of my dad's silver cufflinks. On the inside, I felt an achiness, the body stress from too many pills. Most of all, I felt empty—truly and utterly empty—an emptiness I could no longer seem to fill with drugs.

I went to work and spent much of the day thinking about death. I thought of my father's death mostly, but I imagined my own death. I thought about how it would be effortless to get high and just jump off the top of my office building. Yes, the impact would instantly kill me. And that would be it. No more suffering, no more grief, no more thoughts of 9/11, or sexual abuse.

I returned to Florham Park, well within my curfew, ate a quick dinner with my grandparents, took a hot shower, and crawled in bed. On the nightstand, I had fifteen blues and eight xannie bars. I stared at the pills for a long time. Then I pulled out my iPhone, opened the Notes application, and wrote a note to my mother.

> *Dear Mom, if you're reading this, I'm probably dead. Even though you have suspected for some time, I wanted to tell you I relapsed some time ago. None of this was your fault. I'm sorry for everything. I love you so much and I am sorry for all the pain I caused.*
>
> *Love always,*
>
> *Matthew*

I couldn't imagine living another day of this shitty life. But I really didn't want to put my mom through more tragedy. She didn't deserve it. Fuck it. I sat up, separated ten blue pills from the bunch, crushed and snorted all of them at once, two fat lines of semisynthetic opioid up my nose. I waited a minute, then swallowed four of the xannie bars.

This would kill the average person.

Me, however, I got a headache, then went semi-conscious. I nodded and drooled, but I didn't die. Probably didn't come close.

When I woke in the morning, I snorted a couple of blues and put the whole thing behind me.

After my dismissal from Credit Principale back in May, I took up with Fossil Capital Investments a few weeks later. This was the first job I was able to score due to an old colleague of my dad's, but it definitely wasn't my most impressive. The gig was commission only, so I didn't earn a cent until I passed my Series 7 exams.

Fossil Capital Investments was started by Dennis Desmond, a former executive at Cantor Fitzgerald, and the man who hired my father years earlier. The term "fossil," at least as it related to stock traders, referred to the late 1990s when equity and bond trading transitioned from old school telephone trades to self-serve online trading. The older guys like Dennis, then on a trading desk, needed to get with the program or shove off. These antiquated-types would sometimes refer to themselves as fossils, conceding they'd be extinct someday, pushed out by younger, tech-savvy traders.

I worked on the bond desk. Like I said, no salary. Not yet.

Jimmy Sweeney sat next to me, an older guy, also a former Cantor Fitzgerald employee, and talked about the good old days, all the people he knew who died on 9/11. The guy rattled off the names, pronouncing each name precisely, not unlike the prayer vigil at my home some fourteen years earlier. It kind of annoyed me hearing him rattle off all these names.

We often got lunch—meaning I went and picked up sandwiches and brought them back to our desks. It's what the new guy did.

After work, we sometimes walked to Penn Station together.

At the end of work one day, Jimmy asked, "Kid, you ready to bounce? Walk with me."

No, I wasn't ready to bounce. I was ready to collect some money owed me and use it to buy oxy. But I didn't have a reason to stay, so I said, "Let's do it."

The Fossil Capital Investment offices were in a mid-tier building at Park Avenue South and Thirty-Third Street. The station was four long blocks away. We strolled up Thirty-First, crossed Sixth Avenue, passed the Starbucks, when Jimmy said, "Check this out. I get into Penn Station this morning. There's this young kid, young-young, less than you. And he's hurting."

"Hurting?"

"Like he's coming off some serious heroin. Some shit, I don't know, from the night before."

"This kid," I said, "what about him caught your eye?"

"You know. Frown on his face. Tired, couldn't stay awake. That look said he thought no one noticed."

I smiled, maybe grunted out a laugh.

Jimmy was tall, six-four, maybe taller, an imposing man. Had the look of a linebacker gone slack, huge belly, flushed face. A man who loved his golf shirts and baggy khakis. I could always smell Pinot Grigio oozing from his pores. But deep down he was a decent guy. Better than decent.

Here's what Jimmy wanted to say. "Kid, you're a fuckup. It's obvious to everyone, if not to you. And Kid [he always called me Kid] I like you, so why don't you put things in reverse and get your life pointed in the right direction?"

I wanted to say, "Thanks, Jimmy. That means a lot to me. I hear you loud and clear, and I wish I had the willpower to make such a U-turn. But between you and me, big guy, I don't."

After the sexual abuse, I had a hard time trusting people, particularly men. I mean, would anyone blame me? I lost my dad on 9/11, and in a desperate search of a father figure, I allowed myself to trust the one person who told me what I wanted to hear and look where it got me. And even with Jimmy and others who were potentially influential, genuine father figures, I shut them down because I was too guarded to let anyone in.

We got to the station and walked down the steps. Jimmy went right. I went left.

I waited for a count of fifteen, did a one-eighty, back up the steps, and stood on the corner of Thirty-First and Seventh Avenue. I pulled my phone and dialed. Time to get some drugs.

I took the train from Penn Station to Madison Station, New Jersey, drove to Newark, picked up drugs, drove back to New Vernon. Day after day.

At Martin Luther King Boulevard and Elizabeth Avenue, I always passed the same homeless man—white, frail, dirty, tattoos covering track-marked arms.

A deplorable human being.

If I stopped at the light, he yelled, "Bro, you got any money?"

I handed him a couple of dollars, a look of revulsion on my face.

I pitied him. I felt bad for him. Where did a man like that sleep at night? What about the cold? Was he safe? Did people mess with him? How could you let yourself get so low?

I wore a suit and tie, drove a nice car, had a nice place to sleep every night.

Yet my daily routine wasn't so different from his.

Wake up, take drugs, work, get drugs, take drugs.

Only difference between us really was that I had my mom to rely on. Who'd this guy have?

Biggie, my new NYC sizzurp dealer, black guy, dreads, fat beard and belly, telephoned, "You ready?"

I said, "I'm out front, 'round the corner."

I stood far outside from Fossil, on Thirty-Second Street, because I didn't want to be seen with Biggie.

I wore a navy suit, tie, and my favorite loafers. Perfect costume for Wall Street. I spotted Biggie, got in his car, and we drove to 125th and Seventh Avenue and parked. Just up the block was the Alhambra Ballroom and Apollo Theater. My outfit didn't impress too many people in Harlem.

We got out, walked to a corner store, bought Sprite to mix with my prescription cough syrup, Dutch cigars to roll blunts with, and candy to eat once we got high. After we got our supplies, we walked three long blocks to the housing authority, Saint Nicholas, the projects. Biggie's building was tall and spare, same as all of the others, fifteen stories, a dirty brick, some small windows, no trim.

I'd traveled from a trading desk to the projects where I would spend the early evening sipping lean, popping pills, and smoking weed with my new best friend and gang-banger, Biggie.

Inside the building, we skipped the elevator, took the stairs to the twelfth floor, a goddamn slog all uphill, turned right a couple of doors down, and arrived at Biggie's apartment. He was an aspiring rapper, with music equipment covering every inch of the place, weed and half-smoked blunts and handguns on the coffee table.

A lanky, tatted-up black man sat on the couch, slumped deep into the cushions. Biggie pointed at the guy. "Matty, Dex."

"What's up?" I said.

Dex didn't say a word.

Biggie said, "Dex, hang here for a bit. Chill with Matty. I gotta make some quick plays." He leaned over and picked up one of the handguns, a Glock 18, I think, big fat thirty-something round magazine sticking out the bottom of the grip.

"You're leaving?" I asked.

"You'll be all right. Dex here keep you safe."

"No worries," Dex said, a deeper voice than I expected for a skinny guy. To Biggie, he said, "Take your time."

I sat on the black leather couch, lifted a half-smoked blunt from the table and lit it and smoked. I handed it to Dex, who took it and held it for a long time. I pulled a bottle of cough syrup from my bag, the one Biggie sold me, poured half the bottle into my two-liter Sprite. I smoked and sipped and smoked and sipped.

I swallowed a Xanax, and sometime later, my legs melted into the couch.

I sat there with my tailored Façonnable shirt, all the way from Nice, France, the sleeves rolled up, my tie loosened, my hair a sweaty mess. Not a care in the world. No thought of leaving anytime soon. I was in a good place. A safe place.

Dex stood and moved to the windows, leaning forward and peeked between the blinds. He stood upright, medium-height skinny dude, didn't look at me, then leaned forward again and looked.

"What do you see?" I asked.

"Checking if any police lurking about." He looked again. "They sometime circle the place." Peeked one last time. "Nothing."

I thought of my uncle Phil peeking through the blinds the first time he sexually abused me at his house. Don't know where that thought came from and couldn't stop it if I did. That's the thing about drugs. It usually made me forget—more like, pretend that none of the fucked-up, traumatic things I endured ever really happened. In my drug state, my dad didn't die. I wasn't a moron who got manipulated by a switch-hitter.

I took a deep breath. I could smell him, Phil's sweaty glands working overtime. I breathed out through my nose several times but couldn't get the stink out of me. It made me sick to my stomach. I couldn't get the images of him out of my head. I imagined his fat bald head going down on me. Fuck. Just like that, I was brought back in time. I closed my eyes and could feel the chills down my spine, praying it would be over soon. Same feeling I had after it happened, again and again. I opened my eyes. Fuck. I looked down at the purple liquid in my cup. The smell of weed engulfed the apartment, and I took it all in, as if it was some sort of magical incense.

I grabbed a blunt, lit it, and inhaled hard. All better.

19

THROUGHOUT MY ADDICTION, I BELIEVED others didn't notice the change in me, the transformation from nonaddict to addict. I convinced myself I looked good, normal, sober. I also believed the lies I told others.

I met with my probation officer in late July.

A friend arrested for drugs and issued a more severe punishment told me his drug test consisted of a mouth swab. I assumed I'd get the same. I could deal with a mouth swab. I did so by acquiring and then drinking a bucket load of detox mouthwash, guaranteed, so the bottle said, to give me forty-five minutes of clean saliva. Just to be safe, I bought a healthy quantity of fake piss.

When I got to the probation office in Dover, I checked in, sat, and waited. Every few minutes, I glanced at my watch. I had twenty, then fifteen, now ten minutes of clean saliva in my mouth.

The receptionist told me to go on in. I stepped inside the office and met my probation officer, a woman, which surprised me. She introduced herself, Mary Drean. She pushed a stack of papers across her desk, asking me to read and sign in four places.

She said, "Basically, what you have there is a long explanation for what happens if you fail your drug test. I can tell you none of it's good."

I spied the mouth swab kit sitting in front of me on the desk.

Mary said, "Are you going to pass this test?"

"Of course."

She patted a folder with a thick stack of papers inside. "I understand you have been cooperative."

"Yes, yes, of course."

"No problems noted here in your file."

"Right."

"Here's the good news. Once you pass the test, all charges will be dropped. How does that sound?"

"I'm grateful, of course."

"Then let's do this." She reached into her drawer and pulled out a small plastic cup with a lid. "Today, you pee in the cup. Cecil here will show you to the bathroom." A man waited just outside the door.

My heart fell. I just realized that I left my fake urine at home. I was screwed.

Cecil and I plodded off to the bathroom. He stood politely off to the side as I peed in the stupid little cup. The guy didn't bother to glance my way. I could be topping off my mini goblet with fake piss, and then I'd have my life ahead of me, with all evidence of my crimes and weed-sniffing German Shepherds and snarky police officers, and sad glances from my mother, all of it wrapped in a bow and dropped down a deep, dark well never to be seen again. But now, that wasn't going to happen.

I finished peeing, put my business back in my pants, zipped. I screwed the lid on the cup. To be a nice guy, I took some toilet paper and rubbed the cup and lid, sort of polishing the thing. A human courtesy—no reason to make Cecil here get my piss on his hands if I could help it.

I handed him my plastic cup, and he went off somewhere and did whatever they do. I sat on a crummy green chair in the hallway for a few minutes, and Mary called me into her office.

She said, "You failed the test."

"I don't know what to say." Suddenly, I could smell piss in the air. I said, "I got high like two weeks ago. I fucked up. I know it. I thought I'd be clean by now."

"I see it all the time," she said. She looked me in the eye. "I don't know if this is a cry for help. You've had months to get clean. But you didn't. Either you don't want to—"

"I want to. I really do."

"Or, you genuinely can't stop on your own." She put what I assumed was the test result inside my folder. She asked, "Which is it?"

"I don't know."

"Let's do this. Come back in August," she looked at her calendar, "on the nineteenth. That gives you about a month to get all the drugs out of your system. You think you can do that?"

"Yes. I can do that," I said.

"If you're clean then, I'll drop the charges. If not, you're going to jail," she said.

I got in my car and snorted four little blue pills. I'd get clean, but I'd start tomorrow, maybe the day after. I did want to be clean. Really. I wanted to stop living a life of shame. I could do it, too. I knew I could. I wanted to move on. I wanted to become rich and famous. I wanted people to want me around. I wanted my family to say I reminded them of my dad. I wanted the life he had, but bigger, better.

I stayed at my grandmother's but needed some time, so I drove to our house in New Vernon, the place empty, everyone still at Long Beach Island with their toes in the sand. I was emotional on the drive home, imagining the penalties if I failed the next test—more probation, community service picking up trash along the side of the road, jail time. I broke down and cried and cried and sobbed and finally forgot why I was sobbing and sniffed and just stopped. I turned on the radio and listened to music.

I got home, sat at the kitchen table.

My mother texted, *How did the test go?*

Still at the probation office. Can't talk. Call you later.

I roamed the empty house. I ended up in the TV room and sat, restless and confused, for about an hour.

I made myself a drink. Bourbon on the rocks. Then I got high.

I snorted eight blues and swallowed three xannie bars.

I paced the house for two more hours. Should I tell my mother the truth? Should I equivocate, evade the direct truth, offer up the impression, a hint, a whiff of truthfulness. Or should I just lie?

I called a drug buddy for some levelheaded counseling. He said, "Go back in a month with the fake piss. It's not an issue."

"You think?"

"Probation Services, they only hire idiots. I wouldn't worry about it."

"I feel like all I do is run from my problems."

"My advice, don't stop."

I rolled a joint and went outside on the back patio.

I looked up in the crystal-clear blue sky, not a single cloud visible. The summery feel in the air reminded me of 9/11. I cried and then pleaded, "Dad, please give me a sign. I need help."

One night, a few weeks before my father died, he sat up in bed and shouted in the dark at something or someone. When my mother opened her eyes, he told her he had seen his aunt Bruna. "There," he said, pointing at the foot of the bed. Problem was Bruna had died some twenty years earlier of ALS, a hateful disease that eats away at the neurons that control muscle movement, eventually shrinking Bruna's muscles until she couldn't speak or swallow or breathe.

I'd never met Aunt Bruna but had seen photos. I remember one in particular of a girl in her twenties with dark eyes, a bright face, a barrette in her hair, leaning forward, gazing off camera, her hair flouncy and pulled back in a vintage starlet kind of way. The photo was taken in 1969, so said Anna, my father's sister, long before high-res megapixel cameras were as plentiful as pennies. The occasion for the photo, if any, no one could remember.

According to my mother, my father felt Aunt Bruna's presence, pleading with her to believe him. She was right there in the room, he insisted. Definitely not a dream. He could prove it by describing her: round eyes, a timid smile showing small teeth, healthy in all ways, her old self before the ALS took hold.

What bothered my father wasn't Bruna so much as the baby she held in her arms, Rita, my father's younger sister, who had died as an infant.

I learned all this well after the fact, of course—fifteen thorny years later.

I don't know, but I believe that experience was a kind of eureka moment for my father. Seeing Bruna or baby Rita or both together changed him.

The following evening, my father suggested he might die soon, in which case he wanted to be cremated, not buried. Insisted on it until my mother relented. "Fine, cremation it is." To hear my mother tell it, she tried to laugh the whole thing off as the ramblings of a man who worked too hard. A man who didn't get enough sleep. She refused to have a rational conversation about burial arrangements with a man who had recently seen a ghost, or ghosts, perhaps one or both sending a message from the afterlife.

He continued this seemingly unnecessary conversation. He talked about how he was unhappy with his job at Cantor Fitzgerald—was thinking seriously of quitting, maybe to pursue something that made him happier, though he never said what that might be.

My father was thirty-eight years old at the time. Even if Aunt Bruna and baby Rita were sending a message, that the message meant to prepare for an early death was ludicrous.

As I was looking up to the sky for answers, I noticed a fly landing on the railing next to me. I stared at the fly. I was a little high—not loopy but high—and it appeared to me the fly stared back at me. We did this, the fly and me, watching each other for the next fifteen minutes. I caught most of it on my phone.

This was my sign.

My mother had done something similar, asked for a sign the day after 9/11, and gotten a similar outcome. She told me she noticed a fly, and as odd as it sounded, the fly, she reasoned, was her sign. This was my father in spirit, communicating, however minimally, from heaven. Telling us we weren't alone and that he was looking over us. That same fly stayed in our house for six months after my dad died. In her book *Messages: Signs, Visits, and Premonitions from Loved Ones Lost on 9/11,* author Bonnie McEneaney talks about spirit messages sent to those left behind. Some of the stories are far more unlikely than my mother's, and now my own, fixation on flies.

When my mother remarried in 2007, we saw another fly conspicuously sitting on the white pillar next to the wedding arbor. When my mom kissed my stepdad, Joe, the fly—my father in spirit form—flew away. To my mom, this was his way of saying he was okay with the whole thing, and he gave his blessing.

Each time a fly showed up in my life, a feeling of peace and tranquility swept over me. At some point, I began addressing the fly as Dad.

I stared at the fly on the railing, thought, *Dad, what do I do?*

I didn't hear anything, but I felt something. Maybe I had the answer in me all along, who knows? I stretched, dropped the lit joint in my hand, stomped on it, picked it up and threw it into the yard, and then walked inside and called Sunrise Detox over in Stirling.

"We have an opening on Friday," the woman said.

"Then Friday it is. Put me on the books."

I called my mother and confessed, admitted all my failings, unleashed a mountain of shit I'd stored up over months or years, and sort of just let it all out in whatever order it wanted to come out. "And," I said, "I reserved a spot at Sunrise this Friday."

She said, "I'm speechless. I'm proud of you. I love you."

Later that day, I called my mother again and said I needed to pick up some Suboxone in Millburn to hold me over until I checked into Sunrise Detox on Friday. And, well, could I have some money?

On Thursday morning, I called her again. "I need more money."

"For Suboxone?"

I put on a sheepish look, one she couldn't see through the phone. "Four hundred."

"You can't use what you bought yesterday?"

"All gone," I said. "I'm sick, Mom."

Only I never bought Suboxone yesterday. I had plenty at home in my desk drawer. I was an addict, and I did what addicts do—I planned to pickle my brain in opioids right up to the moment I walked in the door at Sunrise. To do that, however, I needed more money to buy more pills.

"Matthew...your voice, your behavior, it feels erratic. Odd may be a better word. Tell me you're not high."

"I'm not."

"And you aren't using this money to buy drugs?"

"No, Mom."

"I'll send the money now."

That afternoon, I called my uncle Tony. I told him what he already suspected—I was high more often than not. I sent him the video of the fly I'd recorded the day before. Oh, and I failed my drug test.

It was midday. I was at work on a break, outside on the street, iPhone to my ear as I leaned against a subway station sign.

I fucking hated it when people spoke in that super-calm voice. That's what Tony was doing to me now, his speech low and even, a man in control of his life.

"Tell me about probation," he said. "About the drug test."

"I'm fine."

"Do I need to call Ricci?"

"They gave me a warning," I said.

"They?"

"My probation officer, Mary Drean. 'Don't do it again.' A warning."

"I'll make some calls, see what's going on."

I was tired, worn down, and Tony could hear it in my voice. I said, "You don't have to make any calls."

A long pause. "Listen," Tony said. "We're going to get you some help." When I didn't respond, he said, "It's a beautiful day. Take a moment and look up at the sky. Embrace nature. Breathe it in."

I inhaled the last of my cigarette, dropped it, and smashed the butt into the sidewalk with my shoe. I took a breath and smelled falafels around the corner on Thirty-Second and Park Avenue South and wanted to vomit.

I looked up. All blue sky. Not a cloud in sight. And I started to cry.

There was a small painting in the foyer of my family home. It was a painting of my house with a quote on the bottom right of the picture. The quote was said by my dad to Uncle Sal on July 17, 2001: "Nothing is better than coming home from a day in New York City and sitting in your backyard watching a blue heron nest in the tree overhead." The beauty of our house amazed my father day in and day out. Something so simple, so ordinary, like a bird settling into a tree, made being miserable at work every day worth it to him.

The painting is still there to this day.

After work on Thursday, I set up a deal. Took the train to Madison, drove to Newark, picked up Dre in my Rover, and drove a few blocks as we made the swap. I didn't know where I was going, and I drove down Lincoln, one of the shittier streets in Newark. I was in the most dangerous neighborhood in the state, and for what? Dre handed over ten blues and four xannie bars, a one-night supply if I paced myself. I put the baggie in my pocket, turned onto a dead-end, and ahead of me saw flashing lights. The Newark cops had pulled over a guy—given the neighborhood. My guess was for buying drugs from some undesirable like Dre sitting beside me. Four police cars sat at odd angles, lights flashing. The guy was white, a kid, and stood beside his car already in handcuffs.

I braked hard, my heart pounding. I turned around, drove a couple of blocks east, and pulled over. My hands were shaking. I couldn't handle this shit anymore.

Dre got out, tapped on the hood of the Rover, said, "I'll see you tomorrow."

I looked at him through the open window, not sure if I should be confiding in my dealer, but I still said, "I'm entering detox. Friday. Tomorrow morning."

"You joking. My best customer and you going over to the dark side."

"See you around."

Dre shook his head. "Good luck, Matty."

The thing with Dre was, I felt as if he cared. My drug dealer cared about me.

I gave him money. He handed over a product. We did this daily. Didn't mean he couldn't care. Hell, sometimes we hung out together, sipping lean and smoking blunts. When I hung out with Dre and his girl and their baby boy, I felt as if I belonged.

I walked in the door of my grandma's house around eight, just under my curfew. I saw her standing in the kitchen, a knowing look on her face, and I broke down crying. Her look wasn't disappointment but concern. She could tell I was unhappy, and probably intuited I was up to no good. I hugged her tight, bawled some more.

"It's going to be all right, sweetie," she said.

"I know, Grandma."

She made flank steak for dinner, salad, mashed potatoes.

After, I went to the bathroom and snorted four blues and popped a couple of bars. I collected my clothes from the guest room, kissed my grandparents goodbye, and headed home.

On the way, I listened to the radio. The song "I'll Be Missing You" by Puff Daddy came on, and I turned it up. I listened and cried. I thought of my dad. I thought of him looking down on me and being ashamed of the person I had become. I was ashamed of the person I had become, so why wouldn't he? I felt like an absolute failure. I pulled in the driveway, parked and walked in from the garage, and saw my mother at the end of the hallway. She looked sad—it was the first time I'd seen her since admitting my relapse. We said our hellos, chatted for an awkward moment, and then I walked up to my bedroom.

I crushed and snorted another four blues, popped another Xanax bar.

Then I passed out. I woke up at three a.m. in the midst of withdrawal. How could I be in withdrawal given that I'd just inhaled eleven pills in the last seven hours? I was snorting nearly 700 milligrams of oxycodone and taking up to 26 milligrams of Xanax a day. *A day.* My body needed more. So I snorted another blue and tried falling back asleep. I tossed and turned for the next four hours, got up at seven, threw up, got the chills, felt nauseous. I snorted my last oxy, swallowed my last xannie.

Then I packed a bag for detox.

I walked downstairs, told my mother I was ill, and asked her to drive me. When we pulled into the parking lot at Sunrise Detox, I felt good about the future. This wasn't an oil change. I was ready to start my life over.

20

I SPENT THE LAST WEEK of July locked up at Sunrise Detox. It took every bit of seven days to get the opiates out of my system. The first two nights were the worst—constant withdrawals, random seizures. I was also in full benzo withdrawal, and the Valium didn't do shit. During a whopper of a seizure, one of the stronger techs yanked on my shorts and injected my ass with Ativan.

On day three, I think it was, I finally fell asleep.

I had my own room, an upcharge I was willing to pay for. As it turned out, I got my money's worth. I spent as much time as possible flat as a pancake lying on my bed. When I wasn't trying to sleep through withdrawal, or actually sleeping, I trudged downstairs to retrieve my meds and some food, and then back to my private room and my private bed. Hotshots like me got to keep our cell phones, a bad idea really in that a clever addict could use the phone to plan an escape. I had no desire to escape. Where would I go? Who'd want me around?

I did, however, use the cell phone. Not for calls but to watch an endless loop of 9/11 videos. At some point between videos, I texted Tony, asked about the conversation he had with my father that morning. I punched on the tiny buttons. *What did he say to you?*

We've been through this.

Was he scared?

Your dad didn't scare.

I knew the answers but asked anyway.

Tony texted, *You can get through this. I love you buddy.*

I read the text and cried. Typed, *I love you, too.*

By day five, Sunrise Detox had become home. A couple of years earlier, I'd spent a week here. The staff loved me. I got along with the patients, even the assholes. Did I mention the food prepared by 5-star chefs? Didn't matter to me, of course, since much of the time, I had no desire to eat.

Detox, for me at least, was about chain-smoking and sleeping. When I wasn't smoking, I lay on my bed and day-dreamed. I pictured a life without pills. I imagined myself an ambitious person, scrappy, goal-oriented, the person I was before addiction. Then I'd actually fall asleep, and dream of floating along, a stronger, fitter me, no pain, no withdrawal, and the first thing I'd do is reach for my pills. I'd wake in a funk, sweating, anxious, the last part of the dream still lingering.

I had hours to kill, to talk to myself, so I told myself I wanted a wife—a hottie—kids, house, a good job, all of it. I told myself with a little discipline and hard work, I could achieve these things.

Other days, I told myself not to bother. Do my time, and, once on the outside, make some calls and hook up.

Then, I told myself to grow some balls. Get dressed, open the fucking door, and walk out of this shitshow. I thought how easy it would be. Get to the parking lot, order an Uber, convince the poor guy to take me to Newark, meet Dre, and get high.

On day six, I thought for the first time what I'd do when I got out. Get high.

I had tried detox in the past and it never worked.

Detox was one thing. Staying sober was another. I needed a good twenty-eight-day program, and I knew I needed it. I just didn't want it. I wanted to go home. I wanted to get high.

That's when I convinced myself I wasn't an addict. I mean, I had been, but not anymore. I'd gotten myself addicted, and now I was clean. Case closed. That same day my mother convinced me to sign up for a twenty-eight-day program. My life was stuck in this unnatural loop and I couldn't stop it. I'd think one thing and a moment later I'd think and sometimes do the exact opposite.

"Fine," I said. "I'll go."

"I'm so proud of you."

"But I want someplace in Florida. I want nice weather. I want massages, acupuncture, hot chicks."

"We'll see," she said.

It turned out my insurance company didn't cover out-of-state drug treatment at luxury resorts. Fuckers. I had one choice: Jersey. So I told myself I wasn't doing rehab. Besides, I was fine.

Tony got wind of my change of mind. When he broached the subject, I was ready. I said I wanted to go back to work. Now, not later. I didn't want to put my precious job at risk, the one with zero pay until I passed the Series 7, which was proving tougher than I thought.

He said, "You need a twenty-eight-day program."

"I need to get back to work."

"Fuck work," he said. "You're going."

"I'm not," I said.

"You're an idiot if you don't go. I'll tell you this. You need to do what's going to result in the most success. The way I see it, another month of treatment is it."

Maybe he had a point.

I could hear him breathing into the phone. "If you don't go and you fuck up, I don't want you in my life. Or Luke's. Think about that before you make your decision."

Luke, Tony's son, was my godson.

"Seriously?"

"You're an adult. It's about time you start doing the right thing."

The first week of August, I transferred to Seabrook House in Bridgeton, New Jersey, some two hours south, for a twenty-eight-day stint. The doctors at Seabrook prescribed Zofran to help me eat, but the thought of chewing and swallowing made me nauseous, and for the next twelve days, I couldn't keep anything down. Seabrook House was a private drug treatment center and rehab program. Patients like me spent thirteen grueling hours—8 a.m. to 9 p.m.—in group counseling. Nonstop chatter, and I hated every minute of it.

I walked into the general meeting room. Big space. Lots of uncomfortable chairs. Same room where the women met. Seabrook had a "no talking to the other sex" policy. Rumor had it that some time ago, men and women rehabbed together. Even spoke to each other on occasion. With all that talk, someone got pregnant, and the geniuses at Seabrook added one more policy to an already crowded policy manual.

Most of the chairs faced front. Women sat on the left. Men on the right. Four feet between genders, a gauntlet for the speaker to walk up and down.

Ridiculous or not, I liked the policy. I looked like shit. Felt worse. I didn't have a thing to offer the opposite sex. Best I keep my clever patter to myself and the other numbnuts on my side of the room.

Today was an exercise called "If you knew me, you'd know that..."

Here's how it worked. You share something about yourself, and if others could relate (if they'd done something equally stupid or embarrassing or hurtful), they raised a hand.

When it was my turn, I said, "If you knew me, you'd know I had a friend die of a drug overdose. More than one. And each time it happened, I showed up to the funeral high."

Half the room raised a hand. More than half. What surprised me was that I believed my little transgression was unique, that I was special in some way. I wasn't. I was an addict, and addicts did things like this.

A guy wearing an Aerosmith tee shirt stood. He was my age and tall. He said, "If you knew me, you'd know I was molested as a kid."

A few hands went up.

I turned red.

I did not raise my hand.

Fuck that.

Only me and Phil knew about the abuse, what Phil might call a little "family fun" time. I had exactly zero plans to acknowledge that part of my life to a room full of strangers. In fact, had no plans to acknowledge it to anyone. Ever. Why would I?

I craned my head around. Lots more hands in the air than I first thought. Was sexual abuse and addiction that common? In this room, it was. For close to ten years now, I figured I was a stupid kid who got manipulated. The dumb one in the family without the gray matter to see what was coming. Maybe I wasn't alone.

With three days left at Seabrook House, it was time for me to figure out my next move. My mother was here for the weekend, part of an exit program called Family Matrix, three god-awful days of lectures about the perils of addiction.

On day two of the big event, I talked with Hayden, my roommate. He said his mom wanted him to go to an extended care program called The Granite House in New Hampshire.

"You should come with," he said.

"Me?"

"Why not?"

I got up off the bed and left the room.

As part of the weekend activities, I had to write a letter to my mother. She had to do the same. In mine, I said she probably saved my life the time she found me on the brink of overdose. I even fessed up to being high when I fell asleep at the wheel and crashed my Jeep. I said other things. Mostly, I was excited to get the fuck out of this shithole, and if writing one last letter would do the trick, then so be it.

The next day, I met up with my mother face to face. It was the first time I'd seen her in a month. She looked beautiful—hair down, a light blue top, white pants, a summery look. She started bawling the moment she saw me. She said, "You look so good. Some color in your face."

"I missed you," I said.

"I missed you too, honey."

We found a bench and sat.

She said, "So listen, I've been talking to your brothers." Here she paused, waiting, I suppose, for some angry response. I didn't take the bait. She spoke softly, her head and mouth turned slightly away from me. "We think it best if you go away for more time."

"Another thirty-day rehab. You think I need it?"

"Longer," she said, and waited again, some of that uncompromising mother's confidence returning. "Ninety days. Maybe more."

I was too angry to speak.

She said, "I also talked with Hayden's mom. He's already signed up for a sober house in New Hampshire. She says it's a nice place."

"Are you fucking kidding me?"

"Just consider it."

"New Hampshire?"

"Please, stop shouting at me."

"I won't do it," I said. "I'm gone for a month and now you want me out of the fucking house?"

That's when the tears kicked into high gear, a flood of water turning my mother's pretty face into a mess of runny makeup. "Do you have any idea how hard it is for me? One of your relapses...do you know what that does to the family?"

No, I didn't rightly understand the collateral damage from a relapse, but shit.

She said, "You stay in your room. You get high constantly. I can't take it anymore. I need you to get sober once and for all."

"I can do that," I said. "I can. I am. Look at me. I'm sober."

"Today you're sober, but how long will it last?"

"I'm not fucking going to fucking New Hampshire, so you can kiss that fucking idea goodbye."

"Hayden, your roommate—"

"I know who Hayden is."

"He's been to three separate rehabs this summer. Did you know that? Three. His mother thinks he has a chance in New Hampshire. The doctors here think the same."

"I'm not Hayden!" I shout. "The guy's got no willpower or whatever. I'm not him. I'm not fucking going."

I walked away.

I'm clean. I know why I used—absent father, fucked-up uncle, all of it. Granted, my mother didn't know about the abuse, but she doesn't need to know. I need therapy or a high-dollar psycho-shrink with big ears, or I don't know what. I don't need to be locked away for another ninety days.

I stumbled upon a gazebo nearby, the whole thing painted white, the color of purity, and I sat on one of the rough benches and started smoking one cigarette after the other. By the time my mother found me, I was on my third.

She said, "I really hate that you smoke."

I exhaled a thick line of smoke, my lips puckered. "I'm aware."

I stared at my mother and thought of my father. I wondered what he'd make of all of this. Then I softened, something let go, and just that quickly, I was tired of fighting. Maybe another ninety days wouldn't kill me. Out of the blue, I said it. "I'll go."

She was crying again. "Thank you so much. It'll be good for you. You'll see."

"I said I'll go. So stop, already," I said, glaring at the tears.

A couple of days later, one of the staff handed over my phone. I had a bunch of messages, one from my mother. *I know you don't have your phone, but I wanted you to hear this. At the gazebo, you remember. Behind you I saw a fly on the railing. When you said you'd attend The Granite House, it flew away. I'm so proud of you. Daddy is too.*

Turned out, my father had been there all along.

So after Seabrook, I signed up for a long nine-month stint with The Granite House, an extended care facility—a halfway house in Derry, New Hampshire—for people like me, fresh out of rehab but no way ready for the real world. The Granite House taught ex-addicts like me how to live by a new set of standards, the same standards every other sober person lived by.

If you didn't follow the standards—the rules—at The Granite House, you were unceremoniously booted.

I'd been at The Granite House a month or more, and I was sort of used to it. It made it easy that Hayden was there with me, especially as the anniversary of 9/11 crept up and I wouldn't be home for it. Every year we go to this shrine in Stirling, NJ, which has two of the beams from the Twin Towers and a bell in the middle that rings at the times the planes hit the buildings.

It's always an emotional day, but staying at The Granite House was much more low-key than going to the shrine and dealing with all that shit there. The staff treated me well, allowing me to skip the afternoon requirements and hang out at the house with them while the other guys went to the gym and food shopping. They let me watch TV, which I used to my advantage to watch 9/11 documentaries that would surely be televised on the anniversary. I didn't have access to my cell phone yet, so this was the only way I could watch these videos.

Little did they know this was another addiction I had.

In some ways, I liked The Granite House. Phase I was the first of three phases and the most restrictive, not unlike volunteer prison. We were stuck in the house, the day filled with group meetings, never-ending talks with a sponsor, one-on-one counseling, and a weird mix of activities—basketball, hiking, some others. I was also required to attend a bunch of twelve-step meetings each week. I forget how many. Phase I residents like me had the option of attending a structured meeting or listening to one of the other residents tell their story, and it counted as a meeting.

I liked the stories. I might hear some version of the same thing outside smoking, but you put a guy in a room with everyone watching, and the stories got better, fuller, all the gaps filled in with nuance and emotion.

Friday night, Drew spoke. He was a few years older, heavy and ugly and funny in a way that made up for the ugly. He had this odd sense of humor, a way of moving his body, the movements telling parts of the story you didn't even hear. The story, the jangly body thing—it wasn't a put-on but a part of him, a man who routinely got himself into some crazy shit and was used to talking about it in a funny way.

Before the meeting started, about a dozen guys pulled chairs into a U.

Drew sat in his chair, leaned forward, said, "I had a pretty normal childhood, I guess. I suppose everyone thinks they did. I don't remember much when I was six and seven, those years." He paused and leaned back in the chair, looked about the room. No eye contact, his eyeballs pointed way over everyone's head. "When I was eleven, one of my uncles, not a blood uncle, but some kind of relation, he forced me to suck him off. He was drunk or high, both probably. The next day he said he couldn't remember any of it. The whole night was a blur, he said, and I half-believed him. Then he winked at me, his memory suddenly coming back."

I thought it was a joke. I stared at him, waiting for the punch line.

Drew was unnaturally still, his head down, looking at his feet. "You know what I'm saying. Later, we did some other stuff. That's about it, I guess."

I looked around the room. With Drew, I usually expected to see grins, a few smirks. No one laughed this time—there was not a smirk in sight. The story was not funny. I guess it wasn't meant to be.

After, a bunch of us walked to Cumberland Farms, a local convenience store. Cumbies, we called it. Being allowed to visit Cumbies was a treat, a prize for good behavior. It was just a quarter-mile up the road from The Granite House, a measly five hundred-yard walk, and it felt like freedom.

On the walk, I felt butterflies in my stomach. Halfway there, I thought about telling Drew, fessing up about my own shitbag uncle. I pulled him aside and shuffled about for a moment until we had some distance between us and the others. I said, "You got a smoke?"

He tossed me a mostly empty pack.

I lit the cigarette and I noticed a little tremble in my hand. I said, "Man, I just wanted to tell you thanks."

"Keep it," he said. "I got another pack in my room."

"For back there. Telling your story."

"Oh, that. I've told it before a couple of times. But thanks."

"I know what you went through. I mean, not exactly, but you know. My uncle, he kind of did the same. When *you* said something, I don't know, it surprised me. It gave me some hope."

Drew turned his face on me. "You'd be surprised. A bunch of us went through that shit."

We kept walking and caught up with the others. I'd finally told someone about Phil and me. No details, but I said something. I felt as if a weight was lifted off my shoulders, as if I had been held down for so long. Finally, I was starting to feel free, and I knew I would continue to chase that freedom.

21

BY LATE DECEMBER, I'D PUT in five months of sobriety, and it wasn't all bad.

I'd finally gotten to visit my family for Christmas. I was only home for a few days, but it was still nice to see them all. Everyone telling me how great I looked—a little fib that I appreciated nonetheless. At The Granite House, I had hours to fill between all the meetings and therapy, and I filled it by eating piles of candy and chain-drinking Sprite; then, when the Sprite ran out, I chugged gallons of Gatorade—anything to drown the empty feeling inside. I had color back in my face, maybe, but I was the most overweight I had ever been.

The day after Christmas, I caught my mother alone in the kitchen. I said, "I wanted to say I'm sorry."

"For what?"

"All I put you through. Mostly, for lying."

She turned away and grabbed a couple of dishes and put them in the sink. She stood with her back to me, not moving. When she turned around, she wasn't sad or angry, but rather relieved. She asked, "Last year, the vase. You made that up?"

"I made it up."

"Why?"

"I needed money."

"To buy drugs," she said.

I didn't respond.

"And the computer programs for work? 'The Bloomberg,' I forget what you call it. The camera."

"All lies."

That's when she smiled.

I said, "You knew?"

"You're my son. I wanted you to be safe. I knew something was going on. What I didn't know was how bad things had gotten."

My mom cared about me all along, and I never really thought about it in that way. I never thought about the effect my drug use had on her, or the mental torment she went through worrying about me all the time. I never really gave my mom the credit she deserved. She grieved over my dad's death in her own way...and I dealt with it by watching videos of jumpers and doing excessive amounts of drugs.

That afternoon, I got on the road with Hayden for the long haul back to The Granite House. I'd spent three days with my family and was ready to get back to my new routine.

Six hours later, we crossed into New Hampshire, I-93 heading north, a straight shot to the small town of Derry (birthplace of astronaut Alan Shepard, which the town's people are rightly proud of) and The Granite House. Around ten that evening, we pulled into a Shell station and filled up with gas. I walked into the small store and bought four Red Bulls—two each.

In a way, I wanted to keep driving. I hadn't driven long distance in over six months, and once I arrived back at The Granite House, I had to surrender my keys for what they referred to as a "car blackout" week. I'd get the keys in the morning before driving to work. I had a job at Extreme Sports, a superstore of equipment for hockey, baseball, softball, and lacrosse. I worked in hockey sales. Back and forth, no pleasure drives in between.

I stood near the pumps when my mother called. "Where are you?"

"Getting gas," I said.

"Greg Macklin just called and said you weren't back yet." Greg Macklin, the executive director at The Granite House.

"When did he call?" I asked.

"Just now. Three minutes ago."

"We'll be on the road shortly. We should make it to the house in ten minutes."

My mother said, "Text me when you arrive."

"Will do. I love you."

Hayden and I climbed in the SUV. I said, "Mack called my mom. Can you believe that?"

"Like we're a couple of kids."

"Fucker."

"He thinks we picked up," Hayden said. He pulled the tab on a Red Bull. "Doesn't trust us. Would you?"

I said, "No. Definitely not. But it bothers me that he doesn't. Fuck him."

We pulled up to The Granite House and unloaded our bags. I dropped the car keys with Ed, the recovery support staff (or RSS) member on duty. He said, "Go piss in a cup, you birds."

We took our plastic urine cups, walked to a nearby bathroom, pissed, and left the cups on a low counter in the office. I went to my room and Hayden to his. I began to unpack, already missing home, when someone banged on my door.

"It's unlocked," I said.

Ed opened the door, a serious look on his face. "You got something to get honest about?"

He implied I was fucked. For what, I wasn't sure. "What are you talking about?"

Ed was kind of ugly with a huge belly and skinny arms, not that I was any better. He did something mean with his eyes every now and then. He was doing it now. "Not a time for games, here. Did you drink over the break?"

"No?" I was more confused than angry.

"You popped for alcohol."

I said, "Test it again."

Ed stared at me. "Did you eat anything with alcohol in it? Anything?"

I hadn't thought of that. "I'm not sure. I'll ask my mom. I didn't drink. No alcohol. I swear."

"I've already logged it in. We'll figure it out tomorrow, I guess. Have a good night."

I texted my mother. *Was there any alcohol in the food I ate over break? I just failed my UA. Alcohol. Not good.*

Not in anything I cooked. I'll ask Aunt Anna.

Okay, thanks.

Twenty minutes later, my mother texted back. *Aunt Anna says there was wine in the pork. Not a lot. It should have burned off.*

I'll talk to you tomorrow. I love you, good night.

Then my aunt Anna sent me a text. *Matt, I am so sorry. I had no idea. Please let me know if I can do anything to help. I'll talk to whoever, explain it was my fault. I love you.*

I was told by the staff that they would send my results to a lab in California for processing and analysis. All I had to do was sit tight. For once in my life, I didn't lie about using, and it actually felt good. I knew that one way or another, this would all get figured out.

On Friday, my buddy David wanted to go to Boston for the day. Problem was I didn't get off car blackout until Sunday, two lousy days away. I wanted to drive bad, anywhere, so I thought what the hell? I told the RSS on duty I had to work—so the no-lying gig didn't last long. I got my keys, and David and I jumped in my Rover.

That afternoon, when we returned from Boston, sober mind you, I walked in just as I might from a day at the office.

Harry was on duty. He put up a hand to slow us down. "Where were you today?"

"Work," I lied. "Busy day."

"Let's try this again. You work at Extreme Sports, right? Manchester Road. I want to know if you were there today. Working."

"Yes, I did. I mean, I was."

"Derry is a small town. Word is you weren't there. People saw you and David driving on Broadway."

No point carrying on the ruse if some shitbird had already squealed. "Fine," I said. "I didn't go. David and I drove to the bank. We wanted to get out is all."

Harry didn't believe me but didn't say so. "You know the drill. I document it—Curt will likely shoot you a text."

Curt was my case manager, a man who enjoyed busting my balls. And here I'd given him an opening. I'd broken the simplest rule in the book—don't lie.

Ten minutes later, Harry knocked on my door, pushed it open, said, "Outside Greg Macklin's office. Your presence is requested. The sooner, the better."

"All for lying about work?"

"Take a seat and wait for one of the case managers to show up."

I walked to Mack's office, sat on one of the scruffy chairs in the hallway, and twiddled my thumbs. My mother texted, *Are you back from work?*

How'd you know?

Curt texted me. Then she picked up the phone and called. "He tells me you are being terminated or fired or whatever the term, kicked out of the program for drinking."

This was news to me, but before I could even react, she added, "Now you lie about work."

"I lied about work," I said. "I made a mistake."

"And the alcohol?"

"I'm sober. No reason you should believe me, but it's the truth."

"I want to believe you."

"I was told nothing would happen before we got the lab results from California."

I sat and waited for another twenty minutes. Duncan showed up, also a case manager. I liked Duncan—he was personable, not a hothead. He'd been around and had a roughness about him, more tattoos than I could count. He said, "Let's go into Mack's office."

Once inside, he said. "Look, you keep failing for alcohol. I think it's time to get honest." Apparently, I failed both drug tests on Monday and Friday that week.

I didn't sit, but stood next to one of the desk chairs. "I didn't drink."

"People make mistakes. You don't want to admit it, I understand. We have to kick you out. You can go to NFA for a month. Come back after."

New Freedom Academy was a treatment center affiliated with The Granite House. NFA was a demotion, like returning to the minor leagues. "No way I'm going to NFA."

"Up to you. Best pack your bags."

I packed two bags and a plastic bin that held my meds—an antidepressant and sleep aid—and all my worldly possessions, then walked to the intake area and asked for my keys.

Duncan said, "The Land Rover, says here it's registered to Michele Bocchi."

"That's bullshit. It's registered in my name."

"I can hand the keys to the registered owner. No one else."

We argued for several minutes until one of the other staffers came along and sort of nudged me out the door. On the way out, I threatened to call the police. I held onto my two bags and the plastic bin, and both Duncan and the other guy, I forgot his name, escorted me across the parking lot and over the property line and waved goodbye.

I stood there, sort of on the side of the road, and called Alexander, another addict and former patient at The Granite House. Alexander had also gotten booted from the program. Come on over, he told me, we'd have ourselves a party.

I used my phone to request an Uber pickup. When I got to Alexander's apartment, I smelled weed from the hallway. I got inside and dumped my bags on the floor.

My uncle Tony texted, *I'm driving up tonight. We will figure this out.*

Don't come. I'm fine.

I half-wanted to smoke. I thought about how nice it would be to inhale some nice weed and get really high, especially since I hadn't smoked in months. Nobody believed I was clean, anyway.

The other half of me said it wouldn't help. Besides, I liked being sober. I liked the feeling of being free from drugs and alcohol, and I knew that getting high or drunk would not solve my problems in that moment—they would only get worse if I actually relapsed. It felt good not waking up in withdrawal. It felt good mending relationships with my family and friends. It felt good having a different outlook on life, on the things that happened to me.

Ten minutes later, Tony texted, *Get the fuck out of there. Go to a hotel. Use your head. I confirmed a reservation. The Sleep Inn, Londonderry.* Someone snitched that I was staying with a weed-smoker.

We went back and forth for another twenty minutes. Finally, I texted, *You win.*

I got another Uber and headed to the hotel, ten minutes up the road. As I walked into the hotel lobby, I got a call from Greg Macklin. "I'm sorry. We made a mistake. Come back to the house. We just got the lab results from California. They came back clean."

"Negative," I said.

"That's what I said. Are you sober? Right now, I mean."

"Yes."

"Then come back to the house. I'm sorry."

I called my mother. She answered the phone after one ring. I heard crying on the other end. "Sweetie, I am so sorry."

"It's okay, Mom. I love you."

Turns out I failed the urine test for alcohol because of the over-the-counter pain-relieving gel I put on my back. For weeks prior to the test, I'd smothered my back in gobs of Mineral Ice. The stuff was greaseless and smelled good, and for a few moments, at least, did what it promised. Voila, I failed for ethyl glucuronide, the intoxicating ingredient found in beer, wine, and liquor. And apparently Mineral Ice.

So I stopped using the gel and learned to live with an aching back. That didn't keep the staff from testing me. They only stopped after five separate tests came back negative. That's when Greg Macklin said, "Enough, already. He's not drinking."

I hadn't been home since Christmas.

By February, I was seven months sober. It was time to make amends to those I had harmed, and this was that trip. Return to the scene of the crime, confess my sins, repeatedly, and take whatever flack came my way.

After I spilled the beans to Drew, I dribbled out a few more beans to Brody, my sponsor. I was appropriately cryptic about who did what to whom, but he got the idea. Brody didn't have much to say other than tell your mom.

"Sure, okay," I said.

"Really. Tell her."

"I said I would." A silly lie and Brody knew it.

I'd leave The Granite House on a Monday right after my drug test. Return Friday in time for my next drug test.

The day before the trip, I got a call from my brother Michael. We chatted for a few awkward moments, something we never did over the phone, then he said, "Scotty invited Paul to spend the night at Uncle Phil's."

"So?"

"Don't let him go."

"Is everything okay?" I was naturally concerned my uncle shitgoose was up to his old tricks.

Michael said, "A couple of days ago, I was over at Uncle Phil's. He was checking out my car. It sounded funny. And the guy, I don't even know what to say, he was acting kind of screwy. We're in the garage, the door open so we can see under the hood, and, well. Okay, so he closes the garage door, and even with the stupid light that never works, everything is kind of gray, then he like gets real close to me. We're both leaning over looking at the motor. I don't know what I'm looking at, and I can't see shit."

"What are you saying?" I asked.

"Nothing. I'm not saying anything. Just don't let Paul go."

"In the garage, did something happen? Did he touch you?"

"I already said—nothing happened."

"Did he say anything?"

"I think Uncle Phil is, I don't know," Michael said. "Creepy."

"What exactly did he say? Repeat the words."

"I don't know. That's not why I'm calling."

"Tell me," I said.

"What difference does it make?" Michael shouted into the phone. "Keep Paul away from him!" He hung up.

The conversation pissed me off. I couldn't get a straight answer out of Michael. I already knew Phil was a douchebag, and whatever he did or said to Michael upset him enough to pick up the phone. It had been nine, close to ten years since Phil and me. Did the pedo voodoo ever wear off? I didn't know. Didn't particularly care. What I cared about were my brothers. I refused to let them fall for the same shittard tricks. I called Paul, told him not to visit Uncle Phil's until I got home. Just don't. I had something to tell him, I said. No way I'd tell him anything, but I bought myself a few days.

22

WHEN I GOT HOME TO New Vernon, I made amends to my brothers, grandparents, and some others, for a variety of small-time foolishness I'd pulled—getting high at their houses, using money for drugs, a bunch of other normal addict behavior that required apologies.

On Wednesday, Paul, my mother, and I sat watching TV when I got a text from Uncle Phil. *You're in town. I haven't seen you in a while. Come over.*

Stop texting me.

We can watch a movie.

I texted, *Leave me and my brothers alone.*

What'd I do?

If I find out you talked to any of my brothers again, it won't end well for you.

Meatball, I was just kidding.

No more.

Have a nice time with your family.

Leave us alone.

For the rest of the trip, I avoided Phil and his entire family. The omission was noticeable, at least to my mother. She asked, "Why haven't you gone to Aunt Maggie's to visit? I'm sure she and your cousins would love to see you."

"I've got a lot on my plate."

"You've made a point to see everyone."

I could tell she really wanted me to visit, so I said, "I'll go."

Not going to happen.

The following day, on my way out of town, I stopped to visit my old guidance counselor at Seton Hall Prep, Zach Hunter. We went out to lunch and I told him about my addiction, recovery, The Granite House. Then, without really thinking, I told him about the sexual abuse with my uncle when I was a kid.

Zach was a thoughtful person. He didn't interrupt, didn't frown or make faces when I told him. He sort of looked off to his left, whatever that meant, and up, like pondering something. He said, "Tell your mom. Tell your uncle Tony. It's what I'd do."

"I don't know why I told you," I said. "It just came out."

"It will be hard, but it's something you need to do."

"You're right," I said, but was he? He had no idea what kind of shitstorm that would cause. My mother would be crushed. My aunt Maggie, she'd be...I didn't know what. How do you feel when you discover your husband is a pedophile and prefers to keep it in the family? Though, for all I know, he's been sucking little dicks all over Florham Park.

After meeting with Zach, I'd planned to swing by Tony's to check out his new Lexus. I was running late, so I called. "I hate to disappoint you, but I don't think I can make it this trip."

"Disappoint me? It's all good, dude."

"I have something I want to say. I just talked to Zach here at the Prep, and well, that doesn't matter...." I stopped talking, not sure I wanted to do this.

"Matt, you there?"

"I'm here."

"What is it?" Tony asked. "Something wrong?"

"Yeah, but it's not what you think. Okay. I don't know how to say this. I mean, I know what I want to say. That's not right. I don't even know if I want to say it."

Tony grunted or breathed or did something that said he was impatient with me. I could hear it, a little noise meant to hurry me along.

I said, "When I was a kid, I don't know, say fourteen, Uncle Phil sexually abused me." I paused for a moment, my voice leaving me. I whispered, "It went on for a while. A couple of years, I don't know. I guess that's what I had to say."

Tony exploded. "What? Phil? This is Phil Riona we're talking about? Your uncle Phil. I want to be clear on this before we say another word."

"Yeah."

"Say it again."

"Phil Riona and me, we masturbated together. A lot of times. We did other stuff."

"Dude, why didn't you fucking tell me?"

"I'm telling you now."

"I would have helped," he said. "You should have said—I don't know." The last part was almost inaudible, maybe talking to himself. "Where are you? Doesn't matter. I'm coming to your house. Have you told your mother?"

"I didn't have time. No."

"We'll tell her together. I just left Englewood," he said, "the last place I was with your dad before he died. This may sound crazy, but it's a sign. He wants us to make this right. Together."

Englewood was a town near Fort Lee, a borough at the eastern border of Bergen County, New Jersey, where my father grew up.

I said, "I'm on my way."

We met on the cul-de-sac, just past my house, stood in the cold February air, snow on the ground, and we talked about what to say to my mom. When we were ready, we walked into the house, called my mother into my father's office, and I asked her to sit in the red desk chair.

"What's wrong?" she asked. She was surprised to see Tony.

I couldn't get the words out. I stood next to the window, tearing up.

"What happened?" she said. "Tell me."

Tony said, "Michele, Matthew just told me Phil sexually abused him. It was some time ago, years. I want you to take a breath and let Matthew tell it."

"Phillip junior?" That was Phil's son, my step-cousin.

"No, Michele. Maggie's husband."

She started crying. Horrified, helpless, hopeless, I didn't know exactly what went through her head, but in a way, I knew it was coming. I started it, and now I had to let it come. She stood and walked to me, fell to her knees and grabbed me, the same pose when she told me my father had died, her arms around my whole body clutching me hard, rough, crying loudly. "I'm so sorry, honey. I am so, so sorry. I don't know how I didn't see this."

I said, "It's not your fault." I told her more, some details I didn't initially tell Tony, all of it jumbled, coming out in no order whatsoever.

Tony spoke, his voice unusually calm. "I made a call to the prosecutor's office. Since you're an adult, it's up to you how we proceed."

"I've thought about it," I said. "I want to file a complaint or whatever you do." I hadn't given it too much thought, actually. I was scared, full of so much fear, and I didn't know what would happen if I did this. But, I knew it was the right thing to do, and I needed to face this shit like my dad would have and handle it like a man.

Right then, the mood changed. We were in action mode. We drove to the Florham Park Police and an officer, Lieutenant Joseph Washington, a buttoned-up guy, pressed steel-blue shirt and dark pants with the orange stripe, had me spill the beans, details, dates, who touched who where—all of it.

"We need it to charge him correctly," Washington said.

The lieutenant was thorough and unrushed. When he was done with me, he said Assistant Prosecutor Charlene Robertson would probably want to talk with me. Most likely, she'd want me to call Phil and allow her to record the conversation. Get him on the record.

I was petrified. My heart plummeted to my knees. I did what I always tried to do, what I imagined my dad did on those calls with my mom and Uncle Tony. Put on a brave face and show I wasn't scared.

"I can do that," I said.

On the long drive back to The Granite House, I got a bunch of texts from my uncle Tony. *I'm sorry. I feel bad. I wish I'd known. Not your fault.*

I'd have put a stop to it. You know that, right?

The guilt was palpable, sticky and thick and it oozed up through my iPhone and up into my head. *Again, not your fault.*

The messages came in waves, making it hard to keep my eyes on the road and respond at the same time. In between Tony's messages, my mother started in. *Honey, I want you to know I'm so sorry.*

I know, I texted.

I love you very much. I wish I could do something to take away your pain.

I don't know what I was feeling. Not pain, I don't think. Something else. Something harder to put my finger on, bewilderment maybe. And momentum. Now that I'd opened my mouth, I felt as if I'd hitched my wagon to the wrong horse. Was that the expression? Or a fast horse. Or a runaway horse, horses, a whole team of those big-ass Anheuser-Busch Clydesdales galloping down the block out of control. Everything was moving so fast I hadn't put words to it yet.

One hand on the wheel, the other balancing my iPhone, I thumbed out a quick message to my mom. *I love you.*

By March I'd graduated to Phase III, a transition to independent living, they called it. At this point, you'd better have a job or else, make amends for past wrongs, and run one of the peer-driven groups every now and then.

The second of March was my father's birthday. In honor of the day, I scheduled time off work—playing hooky. I'd loaf about, read, something; I didn't know what. Around ten, Tony texted. *You need to come home. We're meeting with the prosecutor tomorrow.*

I need to get a pass, I texted. *Not sure how long that will take.*

Make it happen today. Figure it out.

Macklin won't be happy.

Send me his number. I'll take care of it.

Minutes later, Greg Macklin called me. "I just spoke to your uncle. I'm happy you're taking care of things. I'm proud of you. Here's the thing—I don't want you traveling alone."

"Why is that, exactly?"

Macklin was a considerate guy. He could have said, "Because I said so," but didn't. Instead he said, "I want to make sure you're safe."

"You want to make sure I don't slip."

"Same thing."

Here I was trying to move past some monumental shit, and I was treated like a kindergartener. "Fine," I said. "Have it your way."

Then Tony texted, *I'm taking an Acela right now from Newark to Boston.* Acela Express was Amtrak's pricey flagship passenger train service downtown to downtown. He texted, *I need you to get to Boston. We'll take the train back together.*

This is ridiculous.

I gave Greg my word.

You don't have to come.

I'm coming as far as Boston, he texted, the messages getting more terse.

I could only push my uncle so far. *I appreciate it,* I texted.

I learned later whatever lawyerly shit he had on his plate, it got dumped or rescheduled. Bad timing in that he'd recently soured on his firm and was thinking seriously of moving on. He'd mentioned it a couple of times—lousy boss, too much goddamn paperwork, gobs of stress—but he only shared surface stuff. I suspected there was more to it. But when he got the call from the Morris County prosecutor that the meeting was on, he put everything on hold and hustled to the train station.

I saw my uncle Tony as decisive, a man of action, selfless in many ways—much like my father.

I packed some clothes, and briefly thought of cajoling someone in the house into driving with me to Boston, about an hour south. Macklin made me swear not to go alone. But at the last minute I pulled my phone, opened the Uber app, and requested a ride.

An hour later, we drove into Boston, Kneeland Street to Atlantic Avenue, hard left and rolled up to South Station.

Before I got out of the car, Tony shot me a text. *Someone landed in front of the train. Massachusetts, someone said, Crocker Street in Mansfield. The entire line is shut down. The train isn't moving anytime soon.*

Can you let Mack know we're together?

Already done.

I found a seat in the South Station terminal and waited. Four hours later, Tony arrived. Because of the backlog of stranded passengers, all Acela Express trains heading back to Newark were booked. Instead, we grabbed an Uber headed for Boston Logan International Airport. In the car, I pulled my phone and looked for flights. I bought us two tickets for the last flight, 8:05 p.m. to Newark. We arrived, sprinted to the check-in to confirm I hadn't screwed up the booking and had a leisurely twenty minutes to get through security. Naturally, one of the TSA screeners, a bland woman with wide hips, pointed at me, said she wanted to look inside my bag. Low and behold, I had a satchel full of protein shampoo, brushless shaving cream, mint toothpaste, pricey eye cream, vitamin-enriched facial moisturizer, and I didn't know what else—I hadn't planned on flying—all of it bomb-making sized. The woman deliberately examined each bottle, gave me a scornful glance, and dropped the bottles gently into a plastic-rimmed trashcan.

My uncle laughed. "You pack more toiletries than my wife." We made our flight, sat, and buckled in.

Tony said, "It's your dad's birthday."

"It is," I said.

And then he told me a 9/11 story, the story of the car.

After my dad died, it took a week or more before anyone mentioned the Porsche, presumably still there in Jersey City, where my father parked it. My mother asked Tony if he'd mind picking up the car. The following day, Uncle Tony and my uncles Rob and Don drove forty-five minutes to the PATH station at Journal Square. When they arrived, the place was on lockdown, police officers strolling about, all with serious expressions on their faces and a mass of yellow tape everywhere. In the far distance, Tony saw smoke and dust hovering over Lower Manhattan, what the news anchors had taken to calling Ground Zero.

Tony was dropped off outside the tape and walked into the parking deck on the main level, with no idea where he was going. The garage was huge. There was no way of knowing where my father parked his car. He found a small office, poked his head in the door, and found an older black woman staring back at him.

She eyed him, said, "The silver Porsche, am I right?"

"How'd you know?" he asked.

"You look just like him." She took a breath, said, "He was always so polite."

She gave him directions.

He walked up a series of steps, glanced left, and there it was—the only car on the parking level. Directly above the Porsche was a bright light shining down on it.

My uncle told me that's when he lost it—some combination of emotions roiling inside him, unstoppable and taking over. He approached the car carefully, touched the silver paint with the tips of his fingers, as if it was some kind of brittle artifact. Eventually, he slid the key into the lock, and opened the heavy door, held the door longer than necessary. He thought about the last time my father had held that same handle in that same way.

He sank into the driver's seat, leaned forward and hugged the steering wheel. He noticed a Poland Spring water bottle in the passenger seat, the green and blue label, half the water gone. He picked up the bottle, flipped the cap, and took a swig. He wasn't thirsty but wanted to touch the same bottle John had touched, to drink from it, feel the water in his mouth.

He started the car, music blasting from the speakers. He imagined his brother on a random Tuesday morning in September, confident and ready to conquer the world. Tony was crying by then, had been for some time, but couldn't recall when the tears started. He put the car in reverse, gently, slowly backing out. He circled the deck, moving at a snail's pace, careful, as if he was borrowing the car, as if John would later inspect it, a ritual my father had performed whenever he loaned out his precious Porsche.

Tony approached the small office, the black woman standing in the doorway.

His cheeks covered in tears. He waved.

She waved back.

23

THE FOLLOWING MORNING, MY MOTHER and Joe and I drove across town to the Morris County Prosecutor's office, all of twelve minutes from the house. The plan was I'd call Phil, get him to talk, and maybe he'd say something incriminating.

My stomach felt as if there were two heavyweight boxers rumbling around inside. I felt like I was going to faint or throw up or I didn't know what.

Just two days earlier, he texted me. *Let's get together and watch a movie.* The sick fuck couldn't get over me. The last time we "watched a movie" was over ten years ago.

We arrived at the county offices, parked, ambled into a nondescript red brick building with lots of small windows with gray trim, a couple of sad-looking dogwood trees near the front door.

Uncle Tony stood in the lobby. Everyone shook hands, some bewildered head shaking, as in—how the fuck did we get here?

We took the elevator to the third floor, and when the doors opened, there was Lieutenant Joseph Washington in his wrinkle-free steel-blue uniform, a gold patch on the front of his shirt with a bulky handgun on his right hip.

More handshaking. Tony said to me, "I'll be right here if you need anything."

I nodded.

"You sure you don't want me to come in with you?" he asked.

"I'll be okay."

Lieutenant Washington said, "It's probably best you don't come in."

I glanced at my mother and then Joe, and then followed Washington down a hallway and into a little room next to the prosecutor's office. The room was meant for kids, abused kids was my guess, toys everywhere, tiny cars and trucks in one corner. I imagined a television episode of *Law & Order SVU*, the cops talking to some sobbing kid, the good cop asking if the kid's daddy touched her inappropriately. There was a massive rug on the floor with a road winding around houses and trees, the image of a blue railroad train chugging across the rug at an angle. I had the same rug as a kid—it was from the Ottomanson Jenny Collection.

Lieutenant Washington introduced me to Detective Timothy Hayes, who worked sex crimes and child endangerment. Both men were all teeth and grins, just a couple of nice guys trying to put me at ease.

I said, "This is weird."

Hayes shrugged. No big deal.

I didn't say it, but what I meant was, here I was, a twenty-three-year-old man, and I felt like a child. A fat baby in a twenty-something body. Not nearly man enough for the big, bad world out there.

Fuck.

Hayes pointed at the only table in the room, a small round faux wood-grained thing, a kid's table. I sat. The seat of the plastic chair well below my knees. The top of the table so close to the ground, I couldn't get my legs under it. Washington and Hayes waited a moment, and then did the same.

A pencil and a yellow legal pad lay there, closer to Hayes than me.

Hayes tapped the legal pad. "While you're on the phone, I might make a note, some detail or direction I'd like you to take the conversation."

"A direction?" I asked.

"Forget that. I'll write a word or two. A question, I don't know. If you can work it into the conversation, fine. If not, don't force it." He pulled a small digital recorder from his pocket. "You ready to do this?"

"Let's get this over with."

I thumbed my phone, dialed Phil. I listened. Hayes scooted his chair closer to mine, put the recorder to my phone.

Phil picked up on the second ring. "Meatball."

"What's up, Uncle Phil?"

"How're you doing, bud? You scared me the other day with that text message."

"It was nothing," I said. "Bad day is all. It's all good."

"So what's up?"

I glanced at Hayes, who leaned forward, elbows on the tabletop, a big man ready to crush the kiddies table, balancing the recorder next to my ear.

I said, "Not much. I just wanted to talk. If you have some time."

"For you, always," Phil said.

"This is awkward. I guess I wanted to say, I mean. Let me start over. What happened between us. All those years ago. It's been bothering me. I need to talk it through."

"What are you referring to?"

"You and me watching movies. You know what I mean."

Hayes scribbled on the pad. *Be more specific.*

I said, "When we watched porn together. And jerked off."

"Hey, let's talk about this in person."

"Now," I half-shouted.

Silence for a long moment. "Are you recording this conversation?"

"Jesus, no."

Phil wasn't his usual self. He was hesitant, guarded. He said, "I was teaching you things. We talked about this. Because your dad passed away. What we did was perfectly normal."

"I don't know, Uncle Phil. I don't think it was normal. I feel like you would do this with other people—other nephews, my brothers, dead father or not."

"Never. The relationship you and I have is special. I would never do it with anyone else."

"The whole thing fucked me up," I said. "I have trust issues."

"This is your ex-girlfriend you're talking about? She fucked you over. That messed with your head."

I raised my voice. "Us jerking off. You making me blow you. That fucked with my head."

"Matt, buddy, are you recording this conversation?"

"Why do you keep asking?"

"Just double-checking."

Hayes was writing on the pad. *More specific. Where did the blowjob take place?*

"That time, at your house. You made me suck your dick."

Hayes scribbled, *Where? When?*

I said, "Uncle Phil. Don't tell me you forgot. I was a fresh-man in high school. We went to your house. You made me blow you. Why did you do that?"

He muffled into the phone. "I don't know, man."

"Or that time at the beach with Francene and Ken? You blew me. I was what, fifteen, sixteen?"

"What about it, Meatball?"

I hated that god-awful nickname. "I had a crush on Francene. You were sucking my dick. You said to think of Francene."

No response.

"You there, Uncle Phil?"

"I'm here."

Hayes wrote. *Tell him that was your favorite part of your rela-tionship.*

I said, "Your mouth on my dick. That time at the beach. That was my favorite part. You blowing me, I mean."

He laughed. "Ah, that was fun. I remember now. You loved that, didn't you?"

"I did."

This went on for fifteen minutes. Back and forth.

Hayes wrote. *What did he like?*

"What was your favorite?" I asked.

"C'mon, you know me."

He has to say it.

"I want to hear it," I said. Your favorite, it was me sucking you, right?"

"You sure you're not recording this?" he asked.

"I'm not." I put on a little kid tone to my voice. Innocent. Naïve. I said, "Tell me. I know it, anyway. That time at your house. I was a freshman. I put your hard dick in my mouth. That was it, right?"

"Yes. Yes, it was."

"I knew it," I said. I glanced at Hayes. He gave me the thumbs up. "I guess I should be going. We'll talk later." We wrapped up the conversation, and that was that.

Hayes said, "Great job, Matt. Phenomenal work."

"Really great work," Washington said, the first words he'd spoken in the last hour.

It was one of the most gut-wrenching, debilitating conversations I ever had to do. The praise felt good, but deep down, I wanted to get the fuck out of this shitty little room and this shitty building with the half-dead dogwood trees outside and go home.

In the hallway, my mother approached. Joe nowhere in sight. Just my mother, her mouth in the shape of a smile, but the overall impression something intensely unhappy. "You don't have to talk about it. Don't have to tell *me*, I mean, if you don't want."

"I know," I said. "Thanks."

She stepped closer, directly in front of me. "How'd it go?"

"You just said I don't have to say."

"I'm your mother.... It went good. Tell me it went good."

"Later," I said. "I want to get out of here."

"Of course," she said and we shuffled slowly to one end of the hallway, side by side, close enough to touch, my mother staring at the side of my face.

"What?" I said.

"Did he say anything? Did he admit, you know, what he did?"

"Give me a minute."

"Right. I understand." After a beat, she said, "But did he?"

"Do we have to do this here?" I looked around me, the walls freshly painted, but all I saw were imperfections, a spatter of paint on the faux wood tile floor, a missed spot there, the intersection where the wall met the floor, a thin seam of unrecognizable crud.

All I could do was nod.

Later that day, I took a flight back to New Hampshire.

On my way to the airport I got a text from my mother, no words, just a photo of a fly. I could tell from the photo where it was taken—the hallway upstairs, just outside my bedroom door.

I couldn't help smiling. My father was watching over me.

Before I left the prosecutor's office, Lieutenant Washington told me they'd arrest Phil the following day. I felt bad, angry, and dishonorable at the same time. By the time I boarded my flight, the dishonorable part had evaporated, and all I felt was impending doom.

The following day Lieutenant Washington called. The arrest was going down, and in five minutes and they'd arrive at a coffee shop near Phil's office. If he cooperated, they'd ask him to drive himself to the police station.

I had a bunch of questions—A coffee shop? The bad guy gets to drive himself to the pound? But I didn't ask. I said, "Thank you for letting me know."

"We'll talk soon."

Then I got a text from Phil.

Did you set me up?

No response.

Then a call. I let it go to voicemail. "Call me, please." His voice was a whimper. "It's nine-thirty-nine. Please call me. Please."

Seconds later another call and onto voicemail. "Come on, man, wake up. We have to talk. Please."

I texted Washington and said Phil had texted me, called twice.

"Ignore him. Don't respond."

For once, I did what I was told.

I sat on my bed and looked at the window and stared at the glass and beyond for a long time. My roommate, Hayden, walked in. "You don't look so good."

"The police, Lieutenant Washington, just called. Well, a while ago. They arrested my uncle. It's over, I guess. That part of it."

"Fuck him."

"Yeah," I said. "Fuck him." Only my heart wasn't in it. I was nervous, and strangely enough, I felt bad for my uncle. Despite all that happened, I felt this weird affection for him. I knew he was a bad person for what he did, and maybe that just showed how deceived I really was, that I could still feel affection for such a sick man. But I didn't want to inflict pain on everyone I loved. I couldn't see my own future, had no way of knowing the next step or the one after that. Aunt Maggie and my cousins, they'd all hate me. I didn't want to be hated.

The prosecutor charged Phil with first and second-degree sexual assault. His name appeared all over the media, local newspapers, and the internet. Our first court appearance was June, where he stood in front of the court and told the world what he'd done. He pled to second-degree sexual assault. In New Jersey, sexual assault was the legal term for rape. My uncle had just pled to rape. No lengthy trial, no witnesses, no awkward moments recounting my story on the stand.

The whole thing didn't last twenty minutes, and for twenty painful minutes, I didn't look at him. Couldn't.

September 15, 2016, the night before the sentencing hearing, I couldn't sleep. I tossed and turned thinking about the morning ahead.

What if Phil got off? He'd pled guilty, but shit, it could happen. I had this foolish notion he'd bribed the judge. She'd stretch out the hearing, and in a surprise move, reverse course and find my pedomagnet uncle innocent.

I messaged Tony and told him about my fears.

That shit only happens in movies, he responded.

When we got to the courthouse, the prosecutor Ms. Robertson, and another lady, led us—me and Tony and my mother and Joe and Nick—to a conference room and gave us the rundown for the next hour or so. A bunch of my extended family was already waiting in the hallway outside the conference room door, but I wasn't ready to see any of them. I was way too nervous, afraid I might say something stupid or nonsensical or ball my eyes out.

Inside the conference room, I sat at one end of the table and sweated. I was going to barf, I was pretty sure. I asked Ms. Robertson, "Do I have to see him?"

"Yes." A woman without subtlety.

"Is my aunt Maggie here?"

"My understanding is she won't attend the hearing."

Then Ms. Robertson stood and led us through this underground passageway from the conference room to the courtroom. When we got to the courtroom door, more family had gathered, grandparents and aunts and uncles. Some other connections, faces I knew.

Nonna hurried up and handed me a handkerchief. "It was your Nonno's. For good luck."

Aunt Anna said, "Your dad will be standing next to you. You'll do great."

I'll do great...like I was twelve, and this was a school play.

We walked inside and sat in the front row. A few minutes later, Phil showed up. I couldn't keep my eyes off of him. In that moment, I was filled with anger. Two, three minutes, I just stared at him. Then the anger was replaced with guilt. Like this whole fucking mess was my fault. Like I should have said or done something to keep this day from happening, and if I could, I'd go all the way back when I was fourteen and conjure a shield that repelled assholes like Phil from getting too close.

What would my father think of all of this? Would he be proud of me? I thought back to my fantasies as a kid of my Arnold dad. He woke up after being hit in the head with something when the building collapsed, and was awake at the bottom of the rubble. Slowly, he would start turning and twisting through the metal and lifting it all above his head. Finally, after so much effort, he broke his way out of the rubble and trudged out of the debris.

Would I even be here if he were alive?

The judge arrived and things moved quickly.

She sat and fiddled with paperwork. "In just a few moments, I'll decide on a sentence. Sexual assault in the second degree is a class C felony, punishable by a prison term of up to ten years. In this case, I'm inclined to consider five to seven."

The prosecutor, Ms. Robertson, stood, stared directly at Phil, big crocodile tears in his eyes, for a long moment, and then turned to the judge, a woman with sad eyes and an oldish haircut—a bob with bangs—and made her case why the pathetic monster on her left deserved a full seven years in prison for what he did.

The judge's expression didn't change. She leaned her head forward to peek at me over her wire-rimmed glasses and wanted to hear what, if anything, I had to say. As I understood it, Phil's stretch in the big house was vaguely contingent on the next few words out of my mouth.

I didn't want to speak but knew I needed to. That said, I spent days preparing a statement. Ms. Robertson offered to read what I'd written in court, but this was something I had to do. I sat in the front pew between my girlfriend, Biz, and my mother. I was ready to barf, yet when Ms. Robertson called my name, I had a surge of confidence, as if my father was standing there next to me. "You can do this, buddy," I could hear him whispering in my ear. He always called me buddy. I pictured him way up high in the north tower after the plane hit the building, smoke slowly filling the office until there was no clean oxygen left to breathe. Saying goodbye to my mom and uncle the way he did gave me an added jolt of inspiration. I could face what was coming head-on, just like he did. I wouldn't cower away from my fears and worries anymore.

Years ago, my grandma Laura had handed me a business card of my father's. An old card, the creases visible, the paper scuffed and yellowed. Jeez, the thing had to be sixteen, seventeen years old. Could have been older. On the front was my father's name in bold dark blue ink, *John P. Bocchi*, and a title, *Managing Director Interest Rate Derivatives*. In the upper right, the name of the firm, *Cantor Fitzgerald*, the word Fitzgerald in a font so frilly you could hardly read it.

I was at her home, summer, two days before my birthday. This was a birthday present, I suppose, or maybe something about my visit sparked a memory, and she remembered the card. I don't know. We were in the kitchen, a small awkward space, white tile on the floor. In the middle of the room, an old wooden table lugged all the way from Brooklyn.

"It's yours," she said.

I took the card and rubbed the surface with my fingertips. I read the words.

She said, "I just found it. In the drawer over there. He gave it to you, I don't know, years ago."

"To me?"

"I think you used to carry it in your pocket. You were just a boy. You probably left it here. No telling how long it's been in that drawer."

I stared at the card then looked up at my grandma, all smiles showing big white teeth, her cheeks shiny in the way old people's faces sort of glistened in a certain light. Giving the card to me made her happy.

"On the back," she said.

I turned it over. My father had written DADDY MOBILE, in all caps, an odd habit of his I'd tried to emulate for many years before finally giving up. Below, he had written his cell phone number and on a separate note attached, SO YOU ALWAYS KNOW WHERE TO REACH ME.

Back in court, the note I had written triggered a hazy kind of flashback. Could have been the wording or more likely it was my father's boxy handwriting, the way the downward stroke of the letter D never met the curved part at the top. The flashback never materialized. Or if it did, it was only a feeling:

My father was loving and compassionate. The business card confirmed it.

So I read:

"I don't know if you thought this day would ever come. I did not imagine it occurring at this point in my life, perhaps ever. It took me years to realize that what happened between us wasn't normal. Normal relationships between an uncle and a nephew, especially given the state I was in, do not consist of what happened between us. Once the truth was evident, that this wasn't my fault, that it wasn't normal, I lived a life of shame, embarrassment, and anger. I believed I didn't possess the traits a man should embody. Whether or not you feel any remorse today, or have felt any in the past, I want you to know what happened to me doesn't change who I am as a person. Your actions will never dictate how I live my life. I want to make sure those close to me, and hopefully others, will never endure what I have. I have nightmares about the actions you forced me to do. I don't think you realize how much you have hurt me, how I lived with the shame and embarrassment, how I never forgot. I no longer give you that power. I've been through a lot and I have persevered. Standing in this courtroom today was just another hurdle for me to overcome."

My mother and Tony read statements. Both noted how much harm Phil had caused everyone, especially me—how he used my father's death to fulfill his own perverted pleasures. I couldn't stop crying. When my mother spoke, I sobbed quietly. When Tony spoke, I went loud and hiccupy, making all kinds of noise. In that moment, Tony reminded me of my father, the way he stood, confident, doing what he had to get justice for me.

It was Phil's turn. He said something that I don't remember, maybe how five years sounded better than seven. *Please. Oh, please.*

Then Phil's lawyer spoke, threw out some lawyerly language suggesting his client should receive, even required, some measure of leniency. The judge didn't bother to look up. When the lawyer finished, the judge spoke in a clear voice, said, "Not only did this young man lose his father on 9/11, but he also lost his innocence." Here, she glared at Phil. "Because of what you did to him. I hereby sentence you to seven years in state prison. I hope that now the victim and his family can begin the healing process."

My mother cried. Tony cried. I cried.

We won. I won. It was finally over. I had made it through the rubble.

24

AFTER COURT, WE DROVE TO the house for lunch. Family and friends were already there when we arrived. I sat outside on the patio, a plate of food in my lap, and looked up into a clear sky. Another beautiful September day. Eerie, how the sentencing hearing had gotten pushed back and eventually scheduled for the second week of September, same week as the 9/11 attacks. Deep down, I never thought this day would come—the demons set free, a weight lifted from my shoulders. I was on the verge of happy tears. The patio was crowded, the kitchen, the hallway, the entire house filled with people mumbling or telling jokes or whatever people did after a sentencing hearing.

I needed a break and walked out to my car, stood leaning against the door. I glanced into the backyard, through the arbor, same view more or less as the time I had spotted my father, then a ghost. I said, "Thanks, Dad."

In the kitchen, Nick came up to me and said, "I'm proud of you. You did great."

"Thanks, I appreciate it."

A moment later, my mother said something similar.

"I love you, too," I said.

Well after lunch, the house now vacant, Tony texted me. *You made me very proud. You reminded me of your dad up there. You did what you had to do. You faced your shit head-on, just like he would have. Love you, dude.*

I replied, *Thank you for everything.*

Several days later, I experienced a moment of clarity. I was happy. Even with all I'd been through. I was happy with myself, my family, with the life I had created. I was most happy to be sober. My life was getting better, *was* better than just a year ago. I was grateful for the change, for a new outlook. Life was a blessing, and I recognized it. I was blessed that people never gave up on me, blessed that I never gave up on myself.

In twelve-step programs, they say that acceptance is the answer. Sounds true enough. I had the hardest time accepting my father's death. My therapist says I'm lousy at describing my feelings, especially when it comes to my father. He's right, of course. Drugs and alcohol numbed me, made me forget, smoothed the rough edges of reality. Why think about loss when you can snort a pill and make it all go away?

Ditto with Phil.

Once the drugs wore off, however, things were worse. Drugs were akin to slapping a Band-Aid over a scar. Remove the Band-Aid and the goddamn scar is still there. For years, I didn't even consider why I was using. Now that I'm sober, I see a kind of raw truth. That what happened to me doesn't define me.

So today, I feel.

I don't take drugs or drink to mask the pain. I take it in, admit it, acknowledge the thoughts booming through my head.

Sometimes I talk it out. And I move on. I've learned to take the good with the bad, the sensational days and the equally shitty days, to accept the crazy rhythm of my life.

After the whole court thing, I moved back home. If anyone asked, which no one did, I'd rehearsed a little explanation. This was a "transition period," I'd say, but everyone knew the move was really just another twenty-four-year-old squatting with his mom in an effort to finally get his shit together.

One night in my room, I saw a small box in the upper corner of my closet, grabbed my desk chair, and climbed up and wrestled the box down. Inside was an old journal, a gift from my uncle Sal, something he'd given me a Christmas or two after 9/11. I opened the journal at random, read what was on the page.

December 27, 2003.

My name is Matt Bocchi. My dad died on 9/11.

He worked in the World Trade Center. I wish he came back.

The writing, I recall, was a kind of release, not unlike writing this memoir, an airing out of all the shit rumbling inside my head.

The box held other things, little possessions of my father's I'd collected after he died. Down near the bottom, I found an envelope with my name on the front, my father's handwriting, all caps. Inside the envelope was a single sheet of paper folded into thirds. The paper was old Cantor Fitzgerald stationary, a watermark near the top, the office address the World Trade Center, a location that no longer existed.

My father had written on the paper:

MATTHEW,

PUT THIS IN A SAFE PLACE!

LOVE,

YOUR DAD

The stationary was wrapped around a two-dollar bill. Jefferson on the front, showing off his wavy blond hair. Why a two-dollar bill? No idea. Was it just an odd gift from a father to a son, or did this specific bill have some link to a bigger story, a story I have long forgotten or perhaps one I never knew? Later, I asked my mother about the significance of the two-dollar bill. She shrugged.

I'd lost the note and the bill years ago, or I thought I had. Now recovered, I had another small piece of his story in my hand, some tangible piece of him to hold onto. If I thought about it, I could picture him scribbling out the message and then folding the paper into thirds, sitting at his large desk in his office on the 105th floor of the north tower, high above the world without a care in the world.

Thinking about me.

I put the bill inside the folded stationary and the stationary inside the envelope and wriggled the whole thing down to the bottom of the box, under a tube of hair gel and a Porsche key ring, more or less where I'd found it. I returned the box to the closet, the top shelf. I pushed it way in the back and scooted some books in front of it, where I'd likely forget about the box for another decade. I imagined I'd rediscover it, open the box, and once again remember my father and smile.

For some reason, I spent the next couple nights looking at 9/11 jumper pictures again. Maybe I was looking for a release, a way to shed some tears over my dad, something I hadn't done since I got sober. I stumbled upon a few pictures of jumpers that were in an Italian blog archive. I found it so ironic that the blog was Italian, and that for the first time in nearly fifteen years, I found a picture of what could have been my dad. A male wearing a light-colored top and dark pants. My mom said he was most likely wearing a tan or grey sweater and black pants.

I was convinced that I'd finally found him. I called my uncle, told him what I saw. His response was what I needed to hear, finally, after all this time.

"Dude, you're letting Phil manipulate you all these years later, from behind bars. Don't let him win. Think of the good memories of your dad. He died a hero, he didn't jump. He wasn't scared. I talked to him—trust me."

The thing is—I read the papers, I read the report, I spoke with my mom. I knew he was in the staircase. Yet, for some reason, I didn't want to believe it all. I still wanted more.

We decided to get the Porsche fixed after it sat in the garage for ten years. The poor thing didn't get driven once in that time. Uncle Tony and I realized what a waste it was to have such a beautiful car just sitting around, let alone a legacy of my father's—one we were still lucky to have.

Most people with sports cars have to prepare them for the winter, hoping for the best in terms of mice and rats eating away at the wires while the car sits idle in the garage. We were expecting the worse—it had been fifteen years. We had the car towed to my dad's mechanic and got a call from him within a few days. Miraculously, no mice had eaten away at the wires or internal parts of the car. They had definitely shown up—there was mice poop everywhere—but they never ate at any of the wires. Go figure. The only thing we needed to replace was the brake pads and the tires.

When the car was ready, Uncle Tony and I went to go pick it up. He started it up and it sounded amazing, the engine roaring. I hopped in the passenger seat, my uncle in the driver's seat. We sped around the windy roads of New Vernon for an hour. I looked at him change the gears with the same gracefulness my dad had, and we made eye contact and smiled.

"This is what your dad would have wanted."

I couldn't help but look out the window and tear up. I was finally free. I came to accept my father's death and have tried my best to move on from it. Not to forget it, but to move on. I may never be able to fully piece together my father's story, and I'm okay with that now.

I faced genuine obstacles in my life—my father's death, an abusive relative, and then I made things worse with my addiction to drugs and alcohol. I repeatedly put my life in jeopardy by willfully wandering into notoriously violent neighborhoods. I look back on my story and smile, sort of shake my head, and I wonder how I survived. There were times I shouldn't have—the copious amounts of drugs I consumed, the gun-wielding drug dealers—and yet I did. I still wonder, what made me so special?

I like to believe all things happen for a reason—a naïve belief, perhaps. Nevertheless, I cling to the cause and effect of a logical world. In my world, I have learned—am learning—to fight my demons one day at a time. To forgive myself and others, to search for my place in the world, to learn from my blunders. The logic of these simple lessons is that the sum of these days make a life.

Some days we are untouched by life. Others, we are pushed and pulled by forces outside our control. On those days, I believe it best to stand our ground and sway. To bend and lean, to wobble, to let time and gravity, and maybe even momentum, work its magic against the obstacles in our path. And when we are ready, when we are strong and clear in our direction, to stand straight and tall, and move slowly forward.

EPILOGUE

IT HAS BEEN THREE YEARS since I finished this memoir, and wow, what a journey it has been. I'm grateful that I never gave up on getting my story published—finally using my dad's persistence for the better.

In early sobriety, I continued to bounce from job to job, hoping in the process that I could continue to fulfill my dad's legacy, or try to at least. I've realized that I don't want to work in finance, or really any other desk job that I seek—*crave* even—societal and familial acceptance from. Sometimes the path we're meant to be on is right in front of us, and when we stop forcing another one, things just fall into place a little. I want to help people and tell my story to schools, families—anyone receptive enough to hear it. And that's what I plan to do. This memoir is the first step in being able to do that.

Life isn't always perfect, and just because I'm sober doesn't mean that I don't have to deal with life on life's terms. Death, family issues, yeah, they're all still there. Coming forward about the sexual abuse shattered my family—and we're still slowly putting the pieces back together. We'll get there one day, I hope.

I continue to fight my demons one day at a time. For years I used drugs and alcohol to fill the void inside of me, but it was a temporary solution to my problems. Being in recovery today, I have a new life ahead of me with endless possibilities. Possibilities I had never dreamed of. When this book is published, god willing, I'll have over five years of continuous sobriety. I take it one day at a time, and that's all I can really do. That's all anyone can do, really.

The best part about writing—this memoir in particular—has been the therapeutic relief I get from it. I no longer look at videos or pictures of jumpers, or 9/11 at all, for that matter. I don't feel the need to. I know my father's story—at least, most of it—and I've realized that consuming that disturbing material doesn't serve me any true purpose. Instead, I focus on my dad's life and the way he lived it. It's what he would want, after all.

The biggest lesson I've learned through it all is to always maintain hope. No matter how bad it seems, no matter how bleak the end may be, don't ever give up and lose hope. It always gets better. I promise.

I've come to realize that acceptance is the key to my problems—an evolving belief, perhaps—but something I do believe nonetheless. So now, that's what I do. I accept. I take the life events I endured for what they're worth, and I fight—sometimes with every fiber of my being—to push through the pain and get through to the other side. And really, that's one of the gifts of sobriety. Without a drink or drug, I don't mask the pain anymore or try to forget. I get to feel today. It's not always pleasant, but it's better to feel something than to feel nothing at all. So, I'll just continue to sway, leaning into life's punches as they come.

I know if I give in and fall, it'll all come crashing to an end.

ACKNOWLEDGMENTS

THERE ARE SO MANY PEOPLE I want to thank, but I will keep it short and sweet.

My father, John Paul Bocchi, for everything you did for me in your short but fulfilled life. I promise to keep your name and legacy alive forever. My mother, Michele Bocchi, for answering my questions, for being one of my biggest supporters, and for never giving up on me. And my brothers, Nick, Michael, and Paul for never turning your backs on your big brother. I love you all.

To my extended family, thank you for sticking by me throughout all the ups and downs in my life and supporting me along my journey. To my uncle Anthony Bocchi—for pushing me to be the best version of myself— and my aunt Ann Bocchi Schwimmer, thank you both for answering countless questions and providing details about my father I never knew or had long forgotten. To Frank and Jeannie Zammataro, thank you for being in my life, and especially for all your help throughout the writing process.

To my friends who stood by me through thick and thin, and to those who read the early drafts of this book, thank you for your honest feedback.

I want to express my heartfelt gratitude to everyone at Post Hill Press, especially Maddie, Rachel, and Devon. Most of all, I would like to thank Anthony Ziccardi for believing in me since that very first lunch in New York City. And finally, to my editors Latham and Anne. Thank you for polishing my work and for insisting I stay true to my voice. You both helped make my dream come true.

ABOUT THE AUTHOR

 Matthew Bocchi began speaking in front of audiences throughout the tri-state area, delivering a message of hope and perseverance. He is in long-term recovery, with plans to continue writing and speaking about inspiration and resilience. Matt currently resides in New Jersey.